Dreams

Dreams

A guide to understanding the hidden meanings of your dreams

Philip Clucas

PRC

Produced 2003 by
PRC Publishing Ltd,
64 Brewery Road, London N7 9NT

A member of **Chrysalis** Books plc

This edition published 2003
Distributed in the U.S. and Canada by:
Sterling Publishing Co., Inc.
387 Park Avenue South
New York, NY 10016

ISBN 1 85648 669 9

Printed and bound in Malaysia

The information in this book is true and
complete to the best of the author's and
publisher's knowledge. All recommendations
are made without any guarantee on the part
of the author or publisher, who also disclaim
any liability incurred in connection with the
use of this data or specific details.

ACKNOWLEDGMENTS

The publisher wishes to thank Kate
Simunek for kindly providing the illustra-
tions in this book (© PRC Publishing). All
photographs and other images were supplied
by Digital Vision, with the exception of the
images on pages 15, 16, 18 and 217
(Chrysalis Images). Thanks to Philip Clucas
for the images on pages 64 (top right), 115
(bottom right) and 151 (full page).

Contents

Introduction

Sleep is a revitalizing element for the body and dreaming serves a similarly important function for the mind. Both are interdependent and without one or the other we quickly become psychologically imbalanced and lose our grip on reality.

Sleep follows a set cycle—a rhythm of about 90 minutes—that progresses through four distinct phases. The first is "light sleep" when our muscles relax, heart rate slows down, and breathing becomes shallow. Next we enter a deeper sleep, in which both sleep-talking and sleep-walking may present themselves. During the third stage of the cycle, body temperature drops by several degrees, and in this phase it becomes difficult to wake the sleeper. The final,

and fourth, stage is the deepest level of sleep, and will last for about 30 minutes. At the conclusion of this "deep mode" we swing back to the first phase of light sleep again, and at this change over of rhythms dreaming is likely to begin.

The mind employs the full range of senses—smell, sound, touch, taste, and sight—during dreaming, but of these the visual stimulus is by far the most active, a fact made apparent by noticeable rapid eye movement (REM) during dreaming. We also know that dreams take place in color, but because of their fleeting nature, only their most important features tend to be remembered, which may not include reference to color.

Today, the dreams we engender are seen as a form of safety valve, in which our subconscious allows us to live out those desires and emotions that remain suppressed by our waking self—that reinforce the sleeper's hopes, fears, and frustrations. Dreams are likely to mirror the sleeper's everyday experiences (however traumatic or trivial) and may dredge the long-distant past for unresolved problems and conflicts. The way our mind chooses to present these themes and images can create an inspirational, or a strangely surreal, world of infinitely variable symbolism and meaning. This book hopes to shed light upon their interpretation, and act as a guide to enable the dreamer to reach a far greater understanding and appreciation of the messages their inner-psyche seeks to send them.

Types of Dream

It is widely accepted that dreams serve many purposes in our lives and despite their varied range can be divided into categories.

Psychological Healing Dreams

This dream may be disturbing or frightening—a bit like a nightmare—but it helps the sleeper to release an emotional blockage that might be rooting them to the past. The psyche, by exposing a deep inner conflict that has become repressed in waking life, clears a space for future growth and change.

Premonition or Clairvoyant Dreams

These may be emotionally charged dreams that seem to display insight into the future that the dreamer may think is paranormal. In reality, the conscious mind picks up many varied prompts about the likely behavior of those we know—especially people we share strong emotional bonds with. These clues are processed by the subconscious in dreams, to reach us as "miraculous" feats of intuition. To imagine a death occurring in a dream is not prophetic—death is often a metaphor used by the subconscious to show a change of circumstance in the dreamer's own situation.

Reoccurring and Sequential Dreams

Events or circumstances that continue to recur within a dream over the course of months, or even years, are generally indicative of a hidden problem that remains unaddressed by the conscious mind. It might present itself as a frightening experience or a shaming incident that has possibly been festering since childhood – often the result of a supposed injustice dating from school days or a parental reprimand and has assumed an unacknowledged importance out of all proportion to the original event. It is often easier to construct psychological barriers to avoid facing painful truths. However, this negative protection must be confronted and removed before the dreamer has the opportunity to advance.

Factual or Daily Life Dreams

These dreams are composed of familiar places, people, and events that we encounter on a daily basis. Emotions are highlighted and the dream can be easily influenced by sounds (a ticking clock or the noise of road traffic) and other environmental distractions. Such dreams are usually simple and factual with little of symbolic significance. They may, however, serve to jog the dreamer's memory, or help absorb the everyday happenings in our lives.

Problem Solving Dreams

This style of dream usually incorporates a "helper" who divulges an important message to the sleeper, often by the use of symbolism and metaphor. It is therefore important to observe and remember what is said, as this will offer guidance in decision-making. The symbolism of the helper (often a personification of self) may also prove instructional and could be a complete stranger—an archetype from what Jung termed the "collective unconscious," or may even take the guise of an animal. Such dreams offer possible solutions to obstacles and problems commonly encountered in waking life.

Compensatory Dreams

Some dreams perform the function of allowing the sleeper an opportunity to experience an unlikely occurrence such as an excessively shy person might imagine making flamboyant advances toward someone of the opposite sex; or a peace-loving individual dream of perpetrating acts of great cruelty and violence. Contrary dreams are seen to help balance our personality by introducing the opposite to what we might reasonably expect. Thus, to temper a mood where excessive good nature reigns in waking life, the psyche may deliberately send a sad dream to counterbalance our emotions. Likewise, in times of grief and sorrow, the sleeper may experience a comically amusing dream to help balance the equation—failings are met with need. This sort of dream is invariably a temporary reaction to an extreme mood.

Physiological Dreams

These are the easiest dreams to interpret, as they are simply a response to external stimuli sensed by the subconscious and which intrude into the dreamscape. To dream that you are thirsty or cold merely represents your physical state and often the sleeper will be deliberately awoken from the dream to get a glass of water or add an extra blanket to the bed.

Nightmares

These are the most emotional and mentally draining of all the dream types we experience, and are discussed in greater detail in the last chapter of the book. Their intention is to underline the importance of some particular ele-ment within a nightmare, by waking the sleeper at the most compelling (frightening) part of the narrative so the fear can also be acknowledged and absorbed by the conscience mind. If the issue that concerns the psyche is resolved, the nightmares will fade away. However, persistent nightmares that cause fatigue and disturbed sleep patterns indicate deep concerns that the unconscious mind can no longer contain. If this occurs it would be wise

to confide your nightmare to a friend or if this has little impact, consult the professional help of a qualified counsellor.

Lucid Dreams

This style of dream is categorized by the fact that the sleeper knows they are dreaming. A lucid dream will feel realistic and the narrative will appear greatly enhanced by intense imagery. They occur when a connection happens between the subconscious and the conscious, enabling the sleeper to gain greater control over the direction and content of their dream.

Despite the strangeness of any dream, it is only a dream. With practice, lucid dreams may be manipulated to encompass wish-fulfilment, problem solving, or the control of fears. The latter cate-gory is particularly beneficial in the case of lucid nightmares, where events that once upset the dreamer can be turned to the sleeper's advantage. Peace can be made with your demons before you awake.

Dream Beliefs Through the Ages

Dreams have been regarded as mysterious and significant since time immemorial and were believed to link the sleeper with the higher powers that held control of their destiny. Throughout history, dreams assumed an awesome significance that mankind has sought to understand and analyze, according to his prevailing beliefs and custom.

The Babylonians divided their dreamlore into good dreams inspired by benign spirits and bad dreams concocted by demons. Their successors, the Assyrians, went a step further, and proposed that dreams were omens that bridged the temporal realm with that of the spiritual.

Egyptian priests thought that the gods revealed their intentions to the faithful during sleep (never to the conscious mind). Like other peoples of the Ancient World, they believed that to receive the gift of prophesy dreams had to be "incubated" (from the latin *incubar*, meaning to lie down) in sanctuaries or shrines, where special dream beds enabled believers to await the arrival of a god, or their emissary, to deliver guidance. Stone monuments still survive at the entrances of Middle Eastern temples as mute testimony to their success.

The Jews, having "but one terrible and almighty god," could countenance no other voice in their dreams but that of Yahweh (Jehovah), and the Old Testament is peppered with dream revelations—notably to Samuel and Solomon. Perhaps, however, the most famous biblical dreamer is Pharaoh. His vision of "seven well-favored Kine (cattle) and fat-fleshed," followed by "seven ill-favored and lean-fleshed," which consumed the first seven, was interpreted by Joseph in the *Book of Genesis*, to be a prophetic warning of seven years of plenty and seven years of famine that was destined to afflict the Kingdom of Egypt.

The Ancient Greeks believed that sleep was governed by Hypnos, the father of Morpheus, god of dreams. Hypnos brought sleep "with but the brush of wing-beat upon the face of a believer." The Romans held that it was necessary to discover the wishes of the gods, and the Emperor Augustus ruled that a person dreaming about the State must proclaim the dream's contents in the marketplace.

Dreamlore and religion seem happy to mix in many cultures. Hindus respect the guidance of "sleeping wisdom" and in Japan shrines for incubating dreams still exist, notably at the Shinto temple at Usa on the southern island of Kyushu. The Emperor's Palace also featured a dream-hall, which had a polished stone incubation bed.

Australian Aborigines have at the heart of their mythology some of the most elaborate dream beliefs. Their legend of Creation centers upon the Dreamtime when sleeping spirits arose and

wandered the earth, shaping the landscape and singing the names of all-things into being, before subsiding once more into sleep.

Native North American tribes believe that sleep reveals the hidden wishes of the soul, and through dreams all things are possible and all mysteries understood. The most vivid dreamer was chosen from among the tribe to be its shaman or medicine man and through his intercession in visionary trances, their good fortune was assured. By dreaming of the "ways and language" of the animals that the tribe hunted, braves gained mastery over and respect for their prey—the buffalo, the bear, and the deer—whose meat, hide, and fur ensured the continuing survival of the tribe.

Creative Dreams and Inspiration

Many artists, writers, musicians, and inventors have gained inspiration and enhanced their creativity by delving into their dreamscapes. The subconscious mind can bring forth ideas that might otherwise be rejected by the waking mind as too bizarre or extreme. By utilizing and controlling lucid dreaming, ideas are allowed to interact with the fertile nature of the unconscious mind, to be selected seemingly at random by the serendipitous will of the subconscious.

Shakespeare's works are littered with allusions to the dreamscape and, one of the best known of poems wrought from the world of dreams, is Samuel Taylor Coleridge's *Kubla Khan*, conceived during an opium-induced sleep. Upon waking, he had two or three hundred lines of a poem memorized in his head and started to write them down. However, after 54 lines he was disturbed by a knock at the door, and upon returning realized that the rest of the poem had vanished from his mind; a caution to all who seek to record their dreams, not only to

Above: William Shakespeare

Above: Robert Louis Stevenson

write down your thoughts upon waking, but to do so without interruption.

After a night spent discussing the supernatural with her brother, Percy Bysshe Shelley, and Lord Byron, Mary Shelley retired to bed and had a powerful dream, which gave the idea for her book *Frankenstein* or *The Modern Prometheus*. Similarly, the haunting metamorphosis of Dr. Jekyll into Mr. Hyde owes its inception to the dreamscape of Robert Louis Stevenson.

Perhaps the most profoundly psychological of work to be evoked by lucid dreaming, which mirrors the dreamscape as few other works have, are the adventures that befall *Alice in Wonderland* from the pen of her creator Charles Lutwidge Dodgson, better known as Lewis Carroll. Likewise, in the world of art, the Spanish surrealist Salvador Dali claimed that his work could only truly be appreciated by the subconscious. His paintings use a photographic reality to depict a bewildering landscape that is at once disconcertingly alien, and yet hauntingly familiar.

Mozart insisted that the best of his compositions came to him in dreams, while the Italian composer Giuseppe Tartini entitled one of his works *The Devil's Sonata* after he recollected a musical trill played on a fiddle by the devil during a dream. In a similar vein, Paul McCartney awoke one morning, went over to his piano, and played the complete tune (not just a few bars) of the Beatle's hit, *Yesterday*.

The Great Dream Analysts

The neurophysiological explanation of how dreams occur—that sensory signals to the mind, during the rapid eye movement (REM) phase of sleep, trick the brain into believing that the sleeper is having a real experience—does little to enlighten us as to why dreaming is so fundamentally important, and the reason for their creativity and rich narrative.

It is suggested that dreams reinforce the process of memory by integrating new experiences into the "store-room" of the mind but over the past century, the great dream analysts—Freud, Alder, Jung, and Perls, to name but a few—have added their own theories to the explanation of how, and more importantly why, we dream.

The Viennese psychiatrist, Sigmund Freud, stressed the role of the subconscious in the life of the individual, proposing that dreams work on two levels. The "manifest," or conscious level and the hidden, or "latent" level. Dreams of sexual and violent desire are expressed in the subconscious (latent level) using symbolism, as to imagine such events unfolding in the rational mind would prove morally repugnant. This formed Freud's theory of our "superego censor," repressing, or disguising, the desires of our conscious mind. He believed that dreams were a form of wish-fulfilment, which in adults was invariably a desire for sexual activity—hence the vast array of dream symbols that Freud associated with subjects, such as the phallus (keys, lighthouses, snakes) or reference to carnal desire (flying, swimming, being impaled).

Alfred Alder was originally a follower of Freud, but later proposed that a desire for control, or "individual psychology," was instrumental in explaining the purpose of dreams. He thought that feelings of inadequacy apparent in childhood are, over the course of a lifetime, replaced by adult goals of success and self-belief. He felt dreams reflect these ambitions and are achieved by the individual's will for power.

Part philosopher, and part psychologist, Carl Jung proposed the idea of the "collective unconscious" to explain the nature of symbolism within the dreamscape. Apart from personal input, he believed that a component of any dream was drawn from a universal symbolic language common to all cultures, and based upon religion, folklore, and mythologies—as if all sleepers use the same building blocks to construct their dreams. Within the collective unconscious, he surmised that powerful archetypes—such as the wise man, the hero, and the fool—emerge in our subconscious to represent aspects of the dreamer's own persona. Their purpose is to teach us what our waking self refuses to accept.

In contrast to Jung, Fritz Perls, the founder of Gestalt

Below: Sigmund Freud, the founder of modern psychoanalysis.

theory, proposed that the objects and characters in our dreamscape are purely projections of ourself; aspects of our own personalities that we fail to acknowledge or recognize. Since we are the authors of our dreams, everything in them must be aspects of "self," which are personal creations rather than collective or universal archetypes.

Calvin Hall, the experimental researcher, discovered in the 1950s and 1960s that the same dream topics occur repeatedly throughout a sleeper's lifetime despite (sometimes profound) changes in fortune and situation. Therefore, he postulated, dreams have the mark of timeless endurance. Hall further established their universal link with aggression, proposing that 50 percent of dreams contain at least one act of latent or actual violence, ranging from feelings of mild hostility, to vicious murder. He discovered that children experience dreams containing twice as much aggression as those of adults, and they frequently imagine being pursued or attacked by animals, most notably, dogs, cats, crocodiles, apes, spiders, and snakes.

Ten Tips for Perfect Sleep and Dreaming

S weet dreams require restful, untroubled sleep, and to encourage this, both mind and body need to be properly rested and relaxed. Here are ten suggestions to help encourage a good night's sleep.

1 The amount of sleep that people need varies enormously. However, not only do we all tend to overestimate the amount of hours per night we should spend sleeping, but we also underestimate the amount of sleep we actually get during a "sleepless night." So, try not to worry if you believe that you receive too little sleep as this is very seldom the case!

2 If you have trouble falling asleep at night, you might not crave sleep because your body simply may not have expended enough physical exercise to encourage relaxation. Also, taking a catnap during the day will interfere with sleep patterns, so never make a habit of daytime sleeping.

3 Before retiring to bed, it is

often helpful to lessen tension with a relaxing massage, a set of simple stretching exercises, or a gentle walk in the fresh air. A warm bath (beware of making it too hot) is also usefully soothing, but avoid taking a shower as this might prove too invigorating.

4 Ensure that you leave at least two hours between sleep and your last meal. Food and the process of its digestion will affect your pattern of sleeping and dreaming—encouraging strange and alarming visions, perhaps even nightmares! If you must eat, make it something light—a piece of fruit or a milky drink.

5 Avoid stimulating a body that is preparing to rest. High caffeine drinks, especially coffee and tea, prolong the time it takes to fall asleep. Alcohol and cigarettes will inhibit the rapid eye-movement stage of sleep when dreaming occurs, and deprive the body of rest.

6 Make sure that your bed is as comfortable as possible. We spend a total of a third of our life on this piece of furniture and it is important that it delivers both a restful environment (the mattress should be firm, but not rock hard) and the best possible support for your body. Ideally, your spine should maintain the same contour as when you are standing upright.

7 The bedroom should be well aired (never stuffy) and neither too hot, nor too cold. A temperature of 60°–65°F (16°–18°c) is generally considered comfortable for sleep. Keep the room dark (light is the natural cue for waking) and muffle any loud noise. Recordings of waterfalls or waves lapping against the shore are a gentle and effective way of blocking-out unwanted sound.

8 Keep a notebook and pencil by your bedside, so if worrying thoughts persistently enter your mind and refuse to leave, you can jot them down and consider the matter closed until you revisit them in the morning. Problems always seem worse in the dead of night—never take your work, or worries, to bed with you.

9 It is best to go to bed about 30 minutes before you need to drift off to sleep. Reading a book will distance your mind from the anxieties of the past day. Only by relaxing and calming your mind can sleep be guaranteed. However, if the reading matter proves too absorbing, swap it for something more soporific!

10 On certain occasions, usually related to stress and daytime pressures, we may imagine that it is impossible to drift off to sleep. If this occurs, do not get further stressed by the thought of missing out on your sleep.

A simple relaxation technique to combat insomnia invariably proves effective. Make yourself comfortable in the bed and imagine your body sinking or melting into the mattress. Tense the toes of your left foot, and hold the tension for a count of five. Release and feel how relaxed that part of your body feels. Likewise, repeat the tension in the toes of your right foot; then take it in turns to tense and release the main muscle groups in your body. Work your way from feet to your calves, thighs, buttocks, and stomach. Similarly, from the fingers, hands, and arms to the chest, shoulders, and neck. Finally, hold and release the tension in your jaw and forehead, appreciating the sensation of released tension in each and every area. The distraction of concentrating upon the exercise, and the relaxation it creates, will probably be sufficiently distracting to lull you to sleep.

Recording Your Dreams

K eeping a dream diary is a useful tool in the quest to interpret your sleeping thoughts. By having a pencil and notepad by the bedside you can, upon waking, jot down whatever you are able to recall about the previous night's dream. At first this may provide only vague, half-remembered glimpses into your dream, but with perseverance and practice you will find that the pathways back to your subconscious become clearer.

Each morning set aside a few minutes upon waking to record your recollections, and by writing them down as an *aide memoire* you will find that other themes and symbols from your dream suggest themselves and are drawn into consciousness. Later in the day transfer the information to a dream diary, specifically set aside to record and explore the dream's original content. I would suggest that in the diary you include the following (or similar) categories:

- Date of dream
- People involved in the dream
- Mood and feelings expressed
- Prominent colors, numbers, or shapes
- What story did the dream enact
- Problems and conflicts encountered
- How the problems were dealt with
- Did the dream occur in the past or the present?
- Prominent symbols
- Repeated elements from previous dreams

• How did the dream end

You may of course feel the need to add, or amend, the list of "prompts" that you include in your dream diary (tailored to those that suit you best). It may also be useful to add a graded system from 1–10, where 1 represents a truly terrifying or alarming dream, and 10 denotes a wonderfully inspirational and uplifting dream. Similarly, you could include a scale for how the dream left you feeling the following day, with 1 being totally exhausted or worried, and 10 representing an exhilarating day of high spirits and contentment. In this manner, high and low points can be monitored, and any emergent patterns assessed. The permanent record of your dream diary will give significant insight into your deepest desires and emotions through which you will gain greater self-knowledge.

The Symbolism of Dreams

The following chapters present a wide and varied range of dream symbolism. Each is commonly reported to analysts or recorded within dream almanacs and the topics are acknowledged to perform important roles within our individual dreamscapes. By studying the relevance of the symbolism our dreams present, we can uncover a great deal of information about ourselves. The trivial, and seemingly innocuous, might offer significant insight into our life, yet national, or international events, can be dismissed by our psyche as irrelevant or unworthy of reflection.

It was the Roman soothsayer Artemidorus, who wrote that "dreams and the visions of sleep are infused into men for their advantage and instruction." However, it should be remembered that, by its very nature, each dream is unique to the individual, and will have a slightly different interpretation depending upon personal, cultural, and emotional circumstances. Thus, no guide to dreams and dream symbolism can ever offer a complete insight, or definitive approach. Rather, you should use the explanations offered in the following pages for the interpretation of a particular subject and combine it with your own circumstances to work out an understanding of the likely significance of the various dream elements encountered by the sleeping mind. In this manner our innermost feelings and creative forces can be confronted and made known, hopefully resolving the problems of our waking life and enriching it by uncovering hidden strengths and talents.

The Dreams

The Animal Kingdom

The whole spectrum of the animal kingdom features in our dreams and each performs an important role in helping to interpret the message that our subconscious mind sets before us. Animals have always been regarded as possessing an insight into the natural world that mankind, hampered by his intellect, has lost. Their close affiliation with nature accords them status as guides from other worlds and as prophets and as interpreters of secret wisdom.

In modern dreamlore certain animals are held to be omens for good, while others forebode the onset of bad luck. The baser elements that we perceive some animals to possess are often transferred by our psyche to symbolize traits in our own character, such as violence, lust, and greed, which must be tamed and suppressed.

Wild Animals

These represent some of the most exciting and ambiguous dream symbols, as there is always the implied element of danger. The lion embodies the valor and might of the animal kingdom, and has been familiar in dreamlore since biblical times, when it was regarded as a symbol of royal authority and benevolent watchfulness. To encounter a lion in your dream denotes personal gain. However, the nature of the beast is paramount as if it is angered; the benign nature of the omen is reversed with the implicit threat that the beast will turn on you.

The "fearful symmetry" of William Blake's "dread beast," the tiger, is another of the big cats whose demeanor dictates the way in which the dream is analyzed. To suppose that you are stalked by a tiger implies that the dreamer should guard themselves against dangers lurking just out of view. To have the beast spring on you is a frightening scenario, but if you can imagine yourself standing your ground and not running away, you should take encouragement as it indicates that even your fiercest adversary will be overcome by your resolve and determination.

Elephants, when encountered in a dream, symbolize strength of character and dignity in old age—reflections of the creatures' build and longevity. It is considered talismanic for business dealings and denotes prosperity. To dream of feeding an elephant foretells that you will elevate your standing within the community by performing charitable acts.

indulgences, or represents disapproval at our tendency to spread gossip and gloat over the misfortunes of others. Apes—being regarded as near to mankind in both appearance and intelligence—are accorded more respect in the symbolism of dreams, and stand for the ability to rise above the base nature of their surroundings, to assume dignity, and generate respect.

To see a wild animal in a cage traditionally symbolizes the death of innocence—a portent that the urksome realities of life will soon intrude upon your own private world. The cage's symbolism of entrapment may echo the dreamer's own repressed or stifled emotions. By graphically depicting images of imprisonment, the psyche hopes to move the dreamer forward to the freedom of a less constricted and controlled life.

Beasts of the Chase

As ancient animals of the chase, both the bear and the boar occasionally feature in our dreams. The bear represents the virtues of strength and bravery. Should you dream you are in a forest and a bear ambles up to talk to you, hold the image dear for it is

In dreamlore, apes and monkeys have assumed an unfortunate reputation for deceit and meddling in affairs that do not concern them. To dream of monkeys denotes a disgust with past

interpreted as a very lucky omen—the creature represents the "genius loci," the spirit of the forest—and has bestowed great honor by selecting you to commune with.

Boars also represent the magical spirit of the woods and for a sleeper to summon one into their dream augurs a period of charmed existence, in which they will be protected from the dangers of the natural world. For this reason the boar is a popular talisman on shields and warrior crests.

As less ferocious creatures of the chase, foxes are seen to rely on running and guile to outwit their human adversary—qualities which are well reflected in dreamlore. Their wily habit and ability to "bend" their surroundings to their own favor make foxes famous symbols of sly endeavor. In dreams they represent those who watch unnoticed and wish you ill—deceitful rivals that are destined to become resolute enemies. A vixen with cubs, denotes twice the amount of trouble.

When compared to the fox, game animals—notably the deer, the rabbit, and the hare—offer encouragement and dreamers should view their presence as lucky omens. The rabbit's renowned

ability to breed, offers the promise of fertility for women and virility for her male companion. Hares are closely associated with the moon goddess (some see a hare in the moon's contours) and they act to redress some of the lustful excesses of their cousin the rabbit by expressing the virtue of romance and the ability to see the magical quality in all things. Deer are also viewed as animals of the spirit. Due to the branching nature of their antlers, stags have become identified with the "tree of life," and are thought to impart an intuitive wisdom to those who seek their company in dreams.

Domestic Animals

Dreams populated with domestic animals and pets have quite a different atmosphere to the wild creatures previously mentioned. Here, we have the familiar creatures of our fields and hearth, whose gentleness grants them a special place in modern dreamlore.

Dogs are seen to exemplify the qualities of loyalty and determination, as befits "man's best friend" and they symbolize the dreamer's wish to balance a desire to win approval with that of maintaining integrity and independence. Cats, on the other hand, have a slightly tainted reputation and in dreams may be considered fickle (possibly because their feline nature makes them such sensual animals) and, because of their hunting habits, are symbolic of cruelty. To dream about a cat displays an independent spirit and since they are so difficult to catch, a love of liberty.

Horses appear prominently in many dreamscapes, as befits their noble qualities of speed and power. Their presence is essentially about energy and how the dreamer chooses to channel it in the pursuit of cherished goals. Horses seen running free in a field foretells a love affair; while to dream of riding bareback on one, indicates the desire to be overwhelmed by the prowess of an ardent lover, but to be thrown from a horse is never auspicious.

Pigs suffer the slander of being lazy and dirty, yet still find favor in our dreams. Their endearing, almost human, nature make them a favored image to express the virtue of fortitude and hope in the face of adversity. They are thought to herald the success of any venture; and to see a farmyard full of piglets is considered a joyous portent for future happiness. On the other hand, sheep and cattle are viewed in a less favorable light. Their ovine and bovine natures offer dull solace and to imagine them grazing in your dream suggest satisfaction within

Animal Villains

This section deals with those animals that, in our waking lives, have the power to paralyze us with the fear of their presence. In dreamlore, however, a far richer picture emerges. As with all animals that we love to loath, the classic villain, the snake, emerges as a creature of diverse interpretation, and infinite contradiction. Their bite can prove deadly, yet twined around a staff they symbolize healing. The snake represents learning yet it is condemned for its role in casting mankind from Paradise. Its seduction of Eve, and phallic nature, make it an obvious choice to symbolize sexual excess.

the confines of the maxim "slow and steady." It is the logic of those who find comfort in the proverb "he whose eyes are raised to the stars stumbles into the mire."

In dreams, an obvious parallel can be drawn between viewing a dead snake and male impotence—whereas, for a woman to imagine a serpent slithering into her bed is taken to indicate a desire for an imaginative and fulfiling sexual encounter. However, if the dreamer is phobic, the portents will be changed to reflect their fear. In these instances the subconscious may be deliberately dredging dark emotions to the surface. This is the shock tactic the sleeping mind employs to focus attention upon a phobia; only by confronting our worst fears may they eventually be conquered.

Another unwelcome visitor to stalk our subconscious is the shark. In popular imagining we see the fin breaking the ocean's surface, the razor-toothed bite, and bloody water, which all combine to make the shark a symbol of dread. Its savage reputation belies the facts. Elephants kill many more people

each year and death within the jaws of a hippo is considered a far nastier and more lingering experience. However, our subconscious thrives on the gothic and displays a seeming delight in parading before us sharks, crocodiles, and spiders to shock us.

To dream of sharks circling around you in the water denotes an adversary that seeks to ambush your successes and pass them off as their own. Imagining that you are being attached by a shark portends that hopes and ambitions will sink without trace. Similarly, crocodiles are said to be omens of foreboding. Their raw primeval spirit speaks to the dreamer of dangers lurking just beneath the surface, and to view them in the dreamscape should alert the sleeper to be weary of fair-weather acquaintances who would gladly crush you if it advanced their own cause.

For many people, spiders are a nightmare animal both in dreams and in waking life. Despite the phobia of many, they are seen in the iconography of dreams to represent the virtues of tenacity and patience. Many cultures consider it extremely unlucky to kill a spider, yet surprisingly, to imagine that you crush a spider in a dream is regarded as a fortuitous event. Even more bizarre is the belief that to swallow a spider will endow the sleeper with a magical way with words —the nocturnal equivalent of kissing the Blarney Stone! The creatures' web is also deeply symbolic. It represents home life and the family, which may surface in the dreamer's psyche as a desire to leave home, yet a reluctance to cut the ties that bind them to it.

Creatures of the Deep

We no longer regard the whale as the "great ship swallower" of legend. Now the leviathan is regarded as the gentle and awe inspiring creature that it truly is. In dreamlore, however, these beguiling giants still carry much of their ancient folk memory. The biblical story of Jonah—spiritually reborn from the belly of a whale—has echoes in dream symbolism, which sees the creature as "the womb of nature," wherein the sleeper may undergo a spiritual journey whose destination (replenished from the store of the unconscious) is to be born anew.

Dolphins are another sea-dwelling mammal much beloved by man. However, despite its fondness for human companionship and joyous sense of fun, to see a dolphin in a dream is considered to foretell anxious times ahead. To view one leaping out of the water cautions dreamers against misinterpreting bad judgment for good intent.

The unusual, and occasionally alarming, appearance of the crab and the octopus make them mysterious aquatic visitors to our dreamscape. The crab's impenetrable shell and fierce claws instruct the sleeper to be wary of those who would use bluster and threats to achieve their own ends. Similar unattractive omens surround the octopus. Its diversionary tactic of constantly moving its tentacles to create confusion cautions against concentrating on just one facet of a problem, lest you lose sight of the whole.

The image of deep water is known to represent unconscious thought and those that live within its domain are accorded special status. In the realms of sleep, fish are considered harbingers of inspiration and creativity and to see them swimming in a shoal indicates that you may possess latent spiritual awareness. To dream of a fish's

eye symbolizes the merits of a watchful and diligent nature. But to imagine that you see a dead fish signifies a worry about the way you communicate and interact with other people. You may feel that your lack of emotional warmth is turning you into the proverbial cold fish.

Individual fish species impart their own meaning for dreamers. Because of its legendary instinct to find distant spawning grounds, to dream of a salmon swimming in a river denotes that the sleeper's home and family life will always remain paramount in their mind, no matter how far they travel. An eel in a dream symbolizes a "slippery" acquaintance—somebody who you dislike and distrust. In folklore large solitary trout were sometimes regarded as guardians of the pool and to dream of these venerable fish offers the encouragement that you will eventually rise to the top of your chosen profession.

Crawlers and Creepers

Animals that progress at their own slow, unhurried pace may not, at first glance, appear to offer much to the pantheon of dreamlore. Their lack of speed suggests a dullness of mind, but this would be far from the truth. The toad's association with witchcraft and the sinister side of life belies its ancient association with wisdom, and the creature was once thought to possess a precious jewel within its head, which enabled it to perceive the sacred in all things. To dream of a toad or frog implies that you must look for the true worth within a person or object, and not be deceived by frippery or first impressions,

As might be expected, to dream of a chameleon suggests that you should learn to blend in a little more and be less confrontational with those in authority over you. Adopt the camouflage of conformity so you can influence events from within.

A dream involving a tortoise dictates that the virtues of patience and fortitude bring their own reward. No such solace may be gleamed from seeing either a snail or a leech, however, as both are considered

house (and even our beds) also invariably share our dreams. To imagine that you are plagued by flies may at first appear to be a petty annoyance, but if the swarm grows it forecasts that your detractors, who individually poise no threat, will unite to cause great trouble.

In dreams, rats and mice often appear as messengers. They take little notice of mankind, and dispense neither favor, nor seek to harm. Dreaming of a mouse or rat standing on their hind quarters looking straight at you denotes the imminent arrival of important news, and to see one scurry swiftly away indicates problems with an over-ambitious venture. If a mouse is viewed in a dream nibbling at the food on your table, it suggests that your easy-going nature is being taken advantage of.

In waking life no animals get

inauspicious omens. Snails are said to denote a liar, or a person with a guilty conscience (perhaps echoing the trail that the creature leaves behind), while leeches forewarn that someone you once trusted is taking advantage of you. They are literally bleeding you dry—from good to bad and from bad to worse.

Unwelcome Guests

Mice and rats; fleas and flies; lice and bugs—those that share our

closer to us than lice, fleas, and bedbugs, and in dreams they are also intimately linked to their human hosts. To dream that your bed is infested with bugs suggests that the sleeper feels jealousy and resentment with a person they consider to occupy a less elevated social position than their own. Fleas are considered to symbolize minor annoyances that, when added together, cause a disproportionately large amount of damage. You may gain revenge, however, as squashing fleas or lice in a dream denotes an unexpected windfall.

Flights of Fancy

Flight represents freedom from earth-bound restrictions. Birds are elevated in dreamlore to charmed messengers of the open skies, often interceding between the mortals and the gods who shape their destiny. Their lightness, speed, and ability to travel to other worlds suggests the sleeper's own spirit or psyche. Birds symbolize personal freedom and to encounter one in a dream may be considered an "elevating" experience that presages greater independence in both thought and deed. Birds on the ground, or held in a cage, may metaphorically have had their

wings clipped, and bereft of the power of flight, are regarded as symbolizing drudgery and constraint.

To see a nest in a dream parallels the circumstances of home life. Nest building indicates a change of abode and to envisage one that contains eggs portends future additions to your family, although not necessarily the birth of a child. To smash a nest or steal eggs from within, shows you have an unforgiving nature and should try to soften your behavior before it alienates

you from those you love. Dreaming of a deserted nest, or one blown down by the wind, is taken as a sorrowful omen, which suggests that past indiscretions and reckless behavior are about to find you out.

The symbolism of the egg has long fascinated mankind, and this interest finds reflection in the realm of dreams. In the study of alchemy, the inner man emerged in a state of perfection from the "womb" of the egg and this symbolism is transferred to the world of dreams, where the egg can be taken to symbolize a search or quest to discover the hidden talents that lie dormant within the dreamer.

Birds of Bright Feather

Dreams involving brightly colored plumage are usually to be taken at face value, representing the wish of the sleeper for a little more color and flamboyance in their waking life. Perhaps the bird that best exemplifies this desire is the peacock, but caution should be exercised when it is seen in a dream lest the pride of the bird's magnificent spread of feathers is seen as vanity. If a woman encounters the bird in a dream, it is taken to mean she will be deceived by a lover whose intentions she has misread, and whose commitment she has overestimated. When heard in a dreamscape, the peacock's shrill call is a clarion cry to consider all aspects of a partner, both

the bad as well as the good, so you do not base your opinion of them on a lustful heart alone.

To imagine you see the darting, bright flash of a kingfisher's plumage in your dreams is a very optimistic omen. The bird is the legendary halcyon of Greek mythology. Much of the bird's ancient kudos attaches itself to its symbolism in dreams. The kingfisher offers the promise of a change of luck, which will always be for the better. Humming birds are also seen as bearers of good fortune, indicating successful trips to exotic lands. However, the colorful arrival of a parrot in your dreams is less fortuitous, as its constant squawking forebodes perplexity, and the inability to concentrate on the job in hand.

Feathered Friends

Some birds are esteemed special friends as we perceive them to possess human traits in their character. The most noble example of this is the belief that in times of want, the pelican feeds its chicks upon its own flesh to keep them from starving. This poignant symbol of self-sacrifice (which in medieval times became emblematic of Christs'

suffering) is symbolized in dreamlore to denote the "ultimate sacrifice"—that the dreamer will go to any lengths to protect and cherish those they love.

Conversely, the cuckoo is considered to possess none of the noble virtue of the pelican. Its lax approach to parenthood and the deceitful way in which it fosters its own eggs upon other unsuspecting birds, ensures that to dream of a cuckoo forewarns of deception in love and marriage and to hear one calling presages misunderstanding and jealousy.

To dream of a swan symbolizes a transformation. Their magnificent snow-white plumage has stood for the virtue of purity since ancient times and they were creatures sacred to the White Goddess, for whom they alone sang, so its "swan-song" was only audible to human ears just before the bird's death.

The swan is seen as an encouragement to dreamers to alow their artistic and spiritual gifts to develop and occur naturally, to let intuition guide you in all things.

A lone signet seen swimming on a lake bears witness to infidelity, while to envisage an injured or dying swan must be taken to council against complacency and self-congratulation. Other wildfowl, the duck and the goose, denote prosperity if the birds are

seen flying towards you. However, if they fly in the opposite direction the omens are reversed.

Dreaming of a swallow heralds the arrival of important news from overseas. If the birds are seen flocking for migration it symbolizes a change in your personal circumstances that has been engineered by hard work and great personal determination. Dreaming of a sparrow indicates an endearingly skittish and engaging personality.

However, to see an ostrich foretells the opposite. You shy away from problems and prefer to "bury your head in the sand," rather than confront them head on.

The dove is a worldwide symbol for peace and reconciliation and in dreamlore it espouses similar ideals. The bird is seen as a harbinger that all is well with the world, and its presence in a dream serves to assure the sleeper that any worries they may have will

eventually prove to be unfounded. To see a dove flying upward in a blue sky until it is lost from view, indicates that you should offer support to someone older and less fortunate than yourself.

Catchers and Cleaners

This section looks at birds of prey, and those that perform the unglamorous, yet necessary, function of ridding the countryside of carrion. Foremost among the prey catchers is the eagle, considered master of all. In native American mythology it represents the sky god who has the power to rise above the world of men, and

with acute vision is capable of comprehending all known things. To dream of an eagle points to a desire for a more holistic approach to life. It encourages the dreamer to discover that earthly boundaries are not an enclosing wall, but a gate leading into a more enlightened realm.

To imagine that a hawk enters your dream sends a message to be on your guard for hazards in your personal life. A strong, watchful eye will be required in matters of the heart as predatory rivals may be set to pounce at the slightest sign of weakness.

Owls were sacred to Athena, the goddess of wisdom, and their habit of sleeping during daylight hours earned them an association with the mysterious world of dreams. However, their eerie screech and ghostly nocturnal flight make their symbolism in dreams somewhat ambiguous. They were once considered harbingers of death, but modern analysis has reassessed this brutal omen and now the bird is almost universally seen to represent the need of the dreamer to seek advice from an older and wiser person, whose council will be anchored in experience.

Foremost among the carrion eaters

are vultures, who (as you may well imagine) have a less then enviable reputation when envisioned in a dreamscape. Their very name is synonymous with ill-omen, and to see the birds circling above you foretells rivals, who gaining strength from your misfortune, are awaiting their moment to pounce. The vulture's function of cleaning up carrion may echo your psyche's wish to expunge some of the dead issues that litter your subconscious mind. Similarly, crows and ravens are also regarded as birds of "black legend," whose scavenging habit earn them a reputation for ill-fortune in the world of dreams. Their death-black plumage and solemn demeanor warn of betrayal and bereavement. If however, you turn from the bird's sight and you have the presence of mind to curse its name,

then the omen will be nullified.

Creatures of the Dust

To see insects scurrying about in your dreams indicates that you have many small vexations in your working life, which you feel powerless to deal with and fear may overwhelm you. However, if the sleeper faces each obstacle as it arises, in a methodical manner, the burden will be reduced to a manageable level.

The ant is a well-known symbol of industriousness, and to see these hard-working creatures in your sleep promises a profitable business venture. If the ants are seen to be swarming, this doubles the potency of the omen. Dreaming of a column of ants walking

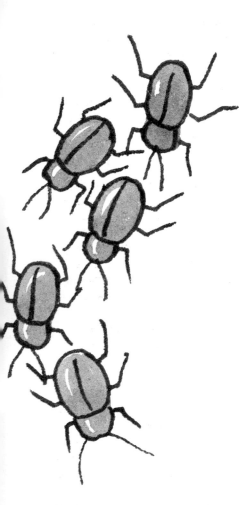

along the ground is another image that offers financial encouragement. Doubtless a reflection of the insect's phenomenal appetite for hard graft and teamwork.

In dreamlore other supposed dwellers in the dust are caterpillars and grubs (although they might more correctly be found on vegetation). Their omens for the sleeper are not encouraging. They signify that you will mix with uncouth and base people who will seek to embarrass you at every opportunity and drag you down to their own unenviable level. The caterpillar can have little comprehension of the transformation that awaits and to dream of a butterfly emerging from the death-like confines of the cocoon into the fragile beauty of its life on the wing is seen as one of the most joyous omens in the world of dreams.

Butterflies symbolize rebirth and the psyche's desire to move forward toward greater spiritual enlightenment. To dream that you see a butterfly flitting from one flower to another indicates the inability of the sleeper to settle down and a yearning to be free from ties and petty restrictions. The butterfly's night sisters, the moths, have a darker side to their dream symbolism. To see a moth flying around the naked flame of a candle has obvious sexual overtones, and the creature's fiery fate serves to alert the sleeper to the perils of rashness in matters of the heart. To see a moth on the wing portends a risky

investment that demands careful consideration, lest you buy experience at too high a price.

Swarmers and Stingers

Dreams where you are seen to be stung signify anxiety and grief caused by your own pigheadedness. If the sleeper is lucky the experience will "prick" them into actions that may remedy their intransigence. As in waking life, wasps are the most likely agents of a sting and to imagine a swarm of the creatures in your dream forewarns that malicious rumors are being spread about you by people you may once have trusted. However, if you see yourself kill a wasp, it suggests you will find an easy and obvious remedy.

In dreams, scorpions represent unforeseen vexations that may be blown-up out of all proportion to their apparent size. It cautions the dreamer that indiscretions you may have committed and wish to keep secret will not simply vanish because they are no longer visible—out of sight is not out of mind. Swarming locusts are seldom a welcome omen in dreams either and (as befits this creature of biblical plague) their presence foreshadows the death of

an enterprise, brought down by the agency of many small setbacks.

The bee is both a stinger and a swarmer, but unlike its fellow insects mentioned earlier, the bee has endeared itself to mankind through its industry, hard work, and the hidden promise of sweetness. In dreamlore they have been symbolic of happiness since time immemorial and are now thought to exemplify the virtues of prudence and courage, which they exercise by staying close to the hive when storms are in prospect and in times of danger defending it with their lives. To dream of bees making honey (especially if the hive is located in an orchard) offers the encouraging prospect of long-term financial reward. However, to accidentally kill or injure a bee indicates the loss of a close friendship.

Plants and Flowers

P lants embody life and are seen to represent the union of the three realms—of heaven, earth, and water. Ancient peoples believed that each species of plant held specific qualities, and this ancestral lore has produced symbolism and interpretation that is still used in dream analysis today.

In mythology, paradise was often thought to be filled with blossom and for every woman living in this world, a flower bloomed in the next. Therefore, blooms assume a feminine persona and in dreamlore stand for feminine beauty and the joy to which the spirit may be raised. To dream of a flower bud about to open represents creation—the manifesta tion of energy moving outward from the center—and the blossoming of an individual through tenderness and love. However, the flower's frailty and imper- manence carry a note of caution, warning to catch life as and when you can, for it does not last very long.

Flowers and Bloom

Flowers startle our senses and remind us of the resonant melodies of nature. Not only does their beauty beguile the eye, but their perfume has the power to evoke long-dormant memories.

Dream images are heightened by scent, and the subconscious mind may use fragrance to remind the sleeper of a distant but important memory. You should try to learn from the emotional response evoked.

In dreamlore, a garland of flowers is viewed as a potent omen, combining the symbolism of the flower with that of the ring. It expresses good luck and fertility and binds together this world and the next. Hence its common use as a funerary wreath.

By common consent, the rose is considered "Queen of all flowers," and to receive a gift of one in a dream is symbolic of being loved, both physically and spiritually. Early records note that roses also denote female sexuality and virginity (the rosebud). Indeed, some dream analysts believe that to look into the crimson-heart of a rose is to awaken our earliest prenatal memory, enclosed within the satin folds of the womb.

In dreamlore, the lily and the orchid stand diametrically opposed to each other, both occupying their own niche but at different ends of the spectrum. Since its earliest associations with the Virgin Mary in Christian iconography, the white petals of the lily have personified supreme purity. The orchid however, with its taint of the "hot-house" and the exotic, has associations with wantonness and debauchery. Indeed, its name *orchis* derives from the original Greek word *testis*, as the plant's fleshy stem was seen to spring from two round tubers. To dream that you pick orchids signifies a lustful encounter, whereas to imagine the blooms wilting and withering represents your present frustration with a sexually unimaginative partner.

The wild iris is named for Iris, the rainbow personified as a goddess, in Greek mythology. The flower, like a rainbow, is both beautiful and reliant upon water and to dream of its golden blooms signifies travel overseas to a destination that may at first glance appear stimulating and exciting, but will soon prove tiresome and prompt fondly remembered thoughts of home. The iris is one of heraldry's most widely known emblems. King Louis VII is said to have dreamed of irises before setting out on Crusade, and he attributed his good fortune in the Holy Land

to the omen. Henceforth the iris, the fleur-de-lis (flower of Louis), was adopted as the emblem of the Royal House of France.

The waterlily, or lotus, is another aquatic flower of great portent in dreams. Its wealth of symbolism in the realms of sleep reflect its sacred nature. It is seen to embody the four elemental forces—earth, from the mud in which it grows; water, from whence it rises; air, in which it reveals the beauty of its bloom; and fire, at the burning heart of its petals. It stands for a spiritual quest, the psyche rising from confusion into the clarity of enlightenment. A note of caution should be sounded, however, as the plant's habit of growing just out of reach also forewarns to keep your aspirations and dreams within reasonable boundaries, lest in striving for impossible goals you end up achieving nothing.

Wildflowers

The purest expressions of joy, wildflowers have no connection with longevity. They bloom and fade to haunt us with their impermanence. As dream symbols they represent the vibrancy of nature. Even the short life of their bloom, and its inevitable dying, serves merely as a reproach against complacency. To dream that you walk along a path flanked by wildflowers is a favorable omen, offering the prospect of romantic fidelity and a lasting union.

Individual wildflowers each have their own meaning within dreamlore. To see a primrose in your dream signifies "love-eternal," while the brightly nodding heads of cowslips speak of childhood innocence and the prospect of a carefree future. Foxgloves have a less favorable reputation and folklore suggests that wily foxes placed the flower-bells on their feet so they could tiptoe around the chicken coop without giving themselves away. This belief is strangely echoed in the world of dreams, where to see a foxglove suggests that the sleeper's willingness to turn a deaf ear will eventually rebound on them. Their insensitive actions and their unwillingness to listen to good advice, will eventually turn friends into enemies.

Buttercups and daisies are traditionally considered the simplest of country flowers and can be seen throughout late spring and summer. To dream of a meadow dotted with yellow and white flowers signifies a soul at ease with itself, and the assurance that the pursuit of pleasures, however humble, will lead to enrichment.

Of all the plants within the iconography of dreamlore, the poppy can claim the closest affiliation. It is the flower of sleep and dreams, whose narcotic qualities are named for Morpheus, the Roman deity who took human form and showed himself to people during dreams. It was once thought that simply staring into the vivid red blooms induced sleep and so its dream symbolism is viewed with some suspicion. The poppy offers the omen of temptation and fleeting happiness. Once picked, the radiant, silky petals are easily shed from the stalk, so to receive a posy of wild poppies signifies impermanence or possibly a brief and unfulfilling romantic encounter.

Harvest Home

Ever since our ancestors learnt to grow and harvest grain seven thousand years ago, the harvest has assumed a vital role in the welfare of man. Harvests were, and in many places still are, a matter of life and death. A plentiful harvest ensured survival, but poor crops could lead to famine and pestilence. Death is usually depicted holding a sickle.

Concern for food production and a successful harvest manifest themselves in our modern dreamscape, as faded echoes from the past. We may not consciously realize that we dream of what earlier cultures called "mother earth," yet dreams of fecundity and plenty still pay homage to her memory. One manifestation of this is the image of the cornucopia, the horn of plenty, whose presence within dreams symbolizes a beautiful realization of your aspirations and desires. However, as with all dreams about harvest, there is an implicit caution to be prudent and to set some of your good fortune aside for less prosperous times.

In the mythology of the Ancient Greeks, ears of ripe corn were considered to be the offspring of the

Sun and the Earth and to dream of a wheatfield ripe for harvest spoke of the inner-fertility of the enlightened mind. In modern dreamlore much of this rich symbolism remains. To imagine you harvest ripe corn indicates good health, while to dream of sowing seed-corn denotes a busy, but financially rewarding time ahead.

A dream of a vineyard, richly hung with grapes, is an omen of a long life, lived to the full. To pick and eat the fruit, however, foretells folly and hardship. This is possibly a reflection of the Celtic folktale that the first grape harvest was gathered by a lion, a lamb, and a hog, and ever since wine had made men be ferocious, mild, and wallow in the mire.

If you see a hopfield in your dreamscape or imagine that you pick and harvest their aromatic cones (used to clarify and flavor beer), it denotes confidence in business ventures, stemming from your ability to grasp and master innovative ideas and inventive propositions. Few plants have a greater aura of mystery surrounding them, and hops can be gathered and made into hop-pillows. These are highly valued as an effective, natural aid to counter insomnia and help induce sweet dreams.

The orchard is another dream image of harvest that foretells the success of ambition. Its glinting, pink or white blossom (following hard on winter's retreat) is a welcome herald of advancing spring. To see boughs laden with the bloom of fruit trees is an enchanting dream omen of happiness and contentment, but not necessarily of permanence. If the orchard hangs heavy with ripened fruit, it points to the consolation that your years of effort and toil will not pass unrewarded.

Trees and Shrubs

Bushes and trees are common dream subjects, and serve to remind the sleeper of their link (literally, their roots) to the natural world. Trees often assume human qualities and can represent our highest aspirations (branches reaching skyward) or basest, earthly desires (the soiled and tangled root). Their leaves are considered to be particularly reliable omens. A green leaf, or one unfurling from the bud, denotes good health. Withered or brown leaves forebode a change in fortune, while dead leaves falling from the bough, or blown into drifts beneath the tree's bare branches, are symbolic of a life being wasted. This is the psyche demanding that the sleeper act more responsibly.

To dream of seeds, either falling from a tree or blowing in the wind, symbolizes growth, or the germ of an idea that, if nurtured, will grow to golden fulfilment. Such opportunities should be seized whenever they occur, as they seldom present themselves again. If the tree's timber is the subject of a dream this shows that through strength, character is developed. To imagine yourself chopping wood bodes well for a contented life, albeit achieved through the strength of your arm and the sweat of your brow. Burning timber indicates admirers: if the wood is too green to light, it denotes a young, inexperienced lover; if the fire smokes, then they will be too old.

Individual tree species have each acquired their own specific significance. The ones featured here are the most important and common species contained in dreams.

The oak is noted for its strength, and to dream of one while pregnant predicts the birth of a healthy, strong-limbed child. The tree is also traditionally associated with the thunder gods, Jupiter and Thor, and statistical evidence indicates that oaks attract lightening strikes more often than any other tree. This may provide one explanation why in dreams it signified fiery temper and a heated argument. An English folktale states that young girls who place acorns under their pillow on the Eve of St. Jude (October 27) will dream of their future partner.

The hazel tree and the hawthorn were both sacred in Celtic mythology (to wantonly fell one was a capital offense) and each is rich in dream symbolism. Hazel catkins, or lambs' tails, seen billowing in the wind, foretell a time of intense joy and to visualize hazelnuts forecasts a period of learning and instruction. But, if the nuts have been partly eaten by an insect or worm, their significance in the dream changes radically. They indicate hopes dashed by malevolent behavior.

Hawthorn was the traditional plant of May garlands and, until Elizabethan times, was gathered while the dew still hung to its leaf, as part of a festival to celebrate renewed fertility.

During the following century, puritan forces declared these country rites idolatrous and the spring revels ceased. However, echoes of the hawthorn's potency still lingers in dreams, where it is held to be auspicious in matters of the heart, indicating a new love affair or an ardent desire reciprocated.

Because of its delicate tracery of branch and leaf, the birch is known as the "Lady of the Woods," and its dream symbolism pertains to the feminine virtues of elegance and grace. The rowan tree, on the other hand, is far less auspicious. Its lustrous red berries appear temptingly edible, but they are in fact toxic and have been linked to poisoning cases in children. They carry the caution in dreams to beware of trickery and deception and to never take things purely at face value.

Evergreens

If deciduous trees are seen to represent the cycle of autumnal death and spring renewal, then the evergreens have an

equally powerful symbolism
of longevity and
immortality. In
funerary rites branches
of yews were placed
alongside the coffin to
represent not the end of life, but
its continuance and the resurrection
to come. However, in dreams the tree
assumes an altogether darker and more
sinister nature. The yew produced the
infamous hebanon used to poison
Hamlet's father, and all aspects of the
tree are toxic. To dream of its somber
shade forebodes an emotional crisis
and to imagine you sit beneath
a yew warns against an
acquaintance, whose constantly
unreasonable and demanding
behavior is slowly sapping you of
your vital essence.

Cone-bearing trees
generally inhabit
poorer, sandy soils,
where their needle-like
leaves are better able to retain
water than their deciduous
rivals. This facet is echoed in
dreamlore, where to see a pine tree (or
another member of the conifer family)
is said to embody the uncomplaining
attitude of
making the
best of what
fate hands you.

To see ivy growing in your
dream is synonymous with physical
wellbeing and financial security,
especially if it grows up the side of a
house. However, its ancient
association with Dinonysos and
Bacchus (respectively the Greek and
Roman gods of wine) make it closely
linked with drunkenness. Thus, to see a

stave of ivy is a strong prompt from your unconscious mind to seek help if you think you have a problem with alcohol. Also ask the views of those you trust and be guided by their honesty—an addicted mind is your greatest deceiver.

Dreams in which sprigs of mistletoe appear, draw deep from a well of ancient mysticism. It was held to be neither shrub nor tree and, without roots in the earth, was thought to have a special association with the divine. Some have claimed mistletoe to be the "Golden Bough" of classic mythology. It was certainly held in awe by the Druidic priesthood and even today its pagan associations make it sit awkwardly alongside the Christian traditions of Christmas. In waking life, mistletoe is seen as a lucky plant and this is reflected in its dreamlore omens, which are almost universally favorable. To dream of gathering mistletoe is said to be symbolic of a change of lifestyle, where new friends and exciting new experiences promise to brighten an existence that might be falling into a rut. To embrace a stranger beneath mistletoe suggests they are destined to become an attentive, thoughtful lover.

with poisonous intent—the devil's bolete, stinkhorn, fly agaric, destroying angel, death cap, and dead man's fingers. In dreams, to encounter them (and it is usually the fairy tale, red-capped variety with white spots that our subconscious selects) denotes unhealthy desires and the pursuit of vain pleasures. To be foolhardy enough to eat one, foreshadows melancholia, humiliation, and disgrace.

Briars and brambles are dream symbols that block our path at each and every turn. Brambles may entangle you with ill luck and are taken to forewarn that trouble is weaving its thorny trail around your best hopes and desires. However, if you imagine that you free yourself from their hold, loyal friends will rally around and support you during a problem and eventually you will emerge victorious.

Stinging nettles are another symbol our subconscious employs to frustrate our progress and alert us to our foibles. To see the plants growing as a barrier

Poisons, Prickles, and Stings

This last section of sylvan dreams concerns those plants that seem to delight in defying us and repay our attention with thorns, with poison, and with stings. Their dream omens are usually just as bad.

Unlike their edible cousin the mushroom, toadstools are seldom, if ever, auspicious when envisioned in a dream. Their very names seem to echo

across your path means you are not wholly in control of your life at the moment and you may need time out to take stock. Being stung by a nettle denotes a period of pessimism and gloom, possibly caused by an untrustworthy friend. However, if you envision the nettles wilting and shrivelling, you can conquer your current adversity and the omens are reversed.

Time, Seasons, and Space

In the realm of our dreams, time and chronological sequence rarely appears as the ordered progression we recognize in waking life. Rather, dream-time follows a serendipitous route, where past, present, and future may be telescoped into a single dream. It is important to try to remember how your subconscious mind presents the time of day or the time of year within a dream as it is always a useful aid to prediction.

To dream of the dawn or dusk—the rekindling or the dying of the light—is always auspicious. Sunrise has long held magical symbolism (personified by Aurora, who rode the glowing orb of the risen sun across the heavens) and in dreamlore the dawn represents a fresh start, the sleeper's escape from their darkest woes. Similarly, to visualize sunset in your dream is also considered fortuitous and is taken to indicate a time of contemplation and a gathering-in of thoughts and recollections. Dusk also symbolizes the psyche's desire for a more spiritual approach to life, as the dying light of conscious day yields to the mysterious night passage of the moon and stars.

The Round of the Seasons

"To everything there is a season, and a time to every purpose under heaven." The words of Ecclesiastes echo the many facets that the seasons of the year personify in dreamlore.

Spring sees the birth of the natural year and is a season of regrowth and reinvigorating energy, when the verdant sap blood of nature returns to the barren land. The season traditionally symbolizes the freshness of youth and the innocence of first love. Spring implies renewed optimism—perhaps a more challenging job or a new romance—where fortune will look kindly upon a resolute heart and bless any enterprise you choose to undertake. However, because spring is seen as the first of the seasons, a note of caution must apply to its dream symbolism, ensuring that you do not let enthusiastic optimism lead you into making unnecessary mistakes.

A dream in which summer appears is indicative of emotional fulfilment and the warmth of human contact. Friends may delight you with a thoughtful

gesture, or a stranger may surprise you with an unsolicited kindness. Each small act appears magnified by the beauty of the season and should be committed to memory as a keepsake against less happy times. To dream of summer appearing unseasonably or unnaturally (perhaps in the grizzled landscape of mid winter) warns the sleeper to guard against relying on luck, when you know that only effort will do.

The fall—Keats' "season of mists and mellow fruitfulness"—conjures up a sense of poetry even in its dream symbolism. From the green softness of its arrival, through golden harvest, to the crimsons and scarlet embers of its dying, the fall draws upon vivid symbolism.

To the sleeper the implication is clear; reap what has been sown and appreciate your blessings before it is too late.

Winter is, as might be imagined, the least portentous of the four seasons. To see this bleak period in your dream proposes a period of contemplation. It is a time to look back on past triumphs and disasters, and try to draw solace from the former and wisdom from the latter.

The Sovereign Sky

The firmament, the celestial vault of heaven, has beguiled mankind since its earliest times and upon its wide canvas, the sun, the moon, and their myriad daughters, the stars, have written man's destiny. The preeminence of the sun as illuminator and life-giver is reflected in its importance in dreamlore, where it is always heralded as an encouraging omen. The sun is taken to symbolize creative energy and the penetrating light of the intellect. For the dreamer, it

the emotional aspect of self. Its constantly changing shape and its wandering course across the night sky establishes the moon as a dream symbol of immortality, rebirth, and the cyclical nature of all things. She is the pale-goddess, the tide-puller, whose waxing to fatness prompts crops to grow and flourish and "maketh the verry earth to sing."

Dream interpretation can sometimes appear irrational, while at other times its meaning seems obvious. To dream of an eclipse falls into the latter category and quite literally suggests that a shadow is about to fall over the dreamer's life. This may indicate personal fears regarding your mental welfare or worries relating to your integrity. Either way, days of storm and darkness may lie ahead.

The planets, stars, and constellation have been considered talismans and lode-stones that have shaped humanity's destiny since earliest times. Dreaming of them represents the sleeper's wish to guide their own fortune, hence "wishing on or striving for a star." The omens are generally good and

represents the opening of a door into a new way of understanding our own unique position within the world of man and the realm of spirit. If clouds are seen to obscure the sun, this foretells unexpected obstacles placed in your path.

The sun's sister, the moon, epitomizes the mysterious nature of the feminine and in dreamlore represents

propose exciting new opportunities, which are eminently attainable if you have the will to believe in yourself.

To view the twinkling of distant star light in the inky blackness of the night sky portends a birth, either physical or symbolic, and to imagine you see a traditional five-pointed star was once thought to indicate that the dreamer was secretly guided by wisdom beyond the reach of knowledge. If the sleeper imagines themselves to be traveling through the boundless infinity of space, it can be at once both unnerving and exhilarating. Such visions predict changes in circumstance that will eventually offer the bright prospect of independence and newly won freedom.

Comets and meteors, when envisioned in sleep, invariably have negative connotations. Their disruptive and unpredictable wanderings in the void of space were said to unbalance the heavens and unsettle the harmony of nature on earth. Little wonder therefore that the appearance of these comets were seldom welcome. In dreamlore the comets baleful influence testifies to shattered hope and wrecked affection. The longer the comet's fiery tail, the longer will be the misery.

Alien Abduction

The human mind, baffled by the wonders of the universe, creates marvels out of that which it cannot rationally explain. This is how the mythologies and legends of our past are born and this is what much of our present preoccupation with "visitors from other worlds" is concerned with.

It would seem unlikely that any dream about alien abduction could be anything other than a nightmare. In dreamlore, however, such imagery is usually interpreted as wish fulfilment. Once concerns for personal safety are banished, and the alien is seen to be benign, the abductee may respond like an overawed child toward an idolized parent.

Features in a Landscape

The Countryside

As might easily be surmised, dreams of the countryside generally bode well for the sleeper. Visions of a gentle, rolling landscape promise solace and contentment. To view green fields and pastures denotes well-being and a feeling of spiritual belonging. This sense of peace may further be enhanced if images of a meadow are evoked. Few places are able to conjure up our childhood innocence better than flower-filled meadowlands. Such dreams have the power to reawaken our earliest memories of youthful rapture and carefree bliss. The dream may, however, carry a veiled warning to enjoy what you have today as the future could offer less joyous times.

If the fields in a pastoral landscape are seen to be ripe with harvest, this suggests happiness. Ploughland indicates success through physical toil but untended crops, seen to be infested with weeds or shriveled by neglect, are considered unfavorable omens that may indicate the dreamer is hiding a secret that might be better exposed.

Fields, paths, and hedgerows combine to make up the familiar, latticed pattern of a country landscape, but individually each has its own distinct symbolism. Paths indicate the progression of a particular goal or project. The longer the path's route, the heavier will be the burden. However, perseverance inevitably brings its own reward and repays the traveller with a sense of accomplishment. Occasionally, such dreams occur at a time when the dreamer is considering abandoning a cherished project that they have been striving to achieve. This should serve as a warning to consider all options and strengthen your resolve. Short paths or narrow, high-sided lanes, indicate aborted opportunity or repressed achievement.

Landscapes with Trees

Trees are common and reoccuring dream images. Just as individual species have their own dreamlore, trees en masse also have a distinctive symbolism. To dream that you are wandering in a dense and shrouded forest may mirror the sleeper's own unease with everyday life. It clarifies a need for personal guidance, where quite literally the dreamer cannot see the wood for the trees. Warnings such as these may be deliberately self-generated to symbolize the shadow side of their psyche.

The confusion of losing your way in a wood or being lost in a forest will generally reflect current personal circumstances, either financial or emotional. Frustration and confusion are exemplified by a thickening of the undergrowth, or getting entangled in briars and thorn bushes, which emphasise the difficulty of the task ahead. Metaphorically the light will be in sight once you have journeyed through the forest and reached the other side.

Jungles offer a more exotic development of the wooded theme. Within their steamy and tropical depths, rich imagery emerges. Encounters with threatening beasts or serpents may signify that you have a rival for the affection of a loved one and to become caught up in dense, creeper-strewn vegetation may be a warning against an ill-advised attachment.

Unlikely as it may seem, to encounter a forest fire in a dream can be regarded as a positive symbol that bodes well for the sleeper. The purging flames makes the forest an impossible place in which to hide. As in nature, where scourging flame is a necessary precursor of regrowth, so the dreamer is left exposed and forced to confront problems in the open, to see them in their true perspective and, hopefully, overcome them.

Deserts in dreamlore represent a similarly exposed landscape, but unlike a fire-ravaged forest, they offer no hope of rebirth, or regrowth. Bereft of any measure of succor, deserts are an unremittingly harsh environment, whose true nature is well reflected in dreams. To struggle across the arid wastes of a desert has long been understood to foreshadow troubled times ahead and is an indication of a desperate need for love and sympathy. The sleeper who imagines dying of thirst, may well experience difficulty coping with the stresses of modern life.

Yet perversely, to dream of seeing an oasis which turns out to be a mirage offers hope for the future and a successful outcome to a problem that may have vexed the dreamer for some time.

Highs and Lows

Mountain or abyss, hill or vale; the extremes of landscape represent fertile ground for dreamers. Depending upon your location, they offer the chance to look down upon mankind or to gaze up above at an seemingly insurmountable height.

As in nature, the mountains of your dreamworld are regarded as obstacles to be conquered. To imagine scaling their heights by climbing to the summit signifies workplace success and advancement—literally reaching the peak of your profession. If, however, you set yourself unrealistic or impossible goals you will dream of climbing but never of attaining height.

To stand on the edge of a precipice denotes concerns regarding the precarious state of a business venture that may need detailed attention or it may indicate that in your private life you should reexamine the character of those you choose to associate with. Imagining that you fall into an abyss signifies the acceptance of the fact that old age is inevitably on its way.

In mythology, mountains and hills are considered to have a thrusting masculine nature. Valleys on the other hand are considered to be protective and are closely linked to the feminine and fertility. These ancient ideals also express themselves in dreamlore, where to find yourself walking through a green and pleasant valley foretells successful parenthood. If the valley is

barren, however, the omens are less predictable and likely to be reversed. Vales cloaked in darkness, or submerged beneath mist, indicate future vexations, where the dreamer may feel trapped in an unsuitable or unrewarding relationship. It would be beneficial for you to review your current situation.

Caves are another feminine feature of the landscape and over the course of history have been seen as portals into an underworld, where intuition and esoteric wisdom hold sway. In dreams, the symbolism of the cave can represent the secret, hidden side of our nature that which we choose to conceal from the light of reason. Thus, to dream of hiding in a cave indicates a failure to come to terms with long-standing issues that we know require our attention, but feel powerless to act upon. The situation is worse if the cave has no apparent exit.

Water in the Landscape

Rivers and streams in dreamscapes represent the life-force and carry potent meaning. Clear, untroubled waters are indicative of strength and purity, but to dream of a stagnant or brackish, slow-moving watercourse may indicate that malevolent forces have been at work and will presently surface to highlight your shortcomings.

To the ancient Babylonians and Egyptians, the size and flow of a river was seen to represent the greater or lesser depth of the dreamer's emotions. Smoothly flowing steams foretold future happiness and prosperity and to encounter turbulent eddies pointed to jealousy and petty squabbles.

Rivers connote the passing of time and in dreamlore their passage is seen to reflect the sleeper's own life course. Straight, swift-flowing waterways indicate honest toil, whereas bends and serpentine curves are seen to represent a happy-go-lucky approach to life, where pleasure is to be found in the most unlikely places.

To dream that you cross a ford is a common theme that has been recorded since antiquity. Usually it occurs when the sleeper is faced with a delicate decision that must be made in waking life. The difficulty in crossing the river—the water's breadth and depth, how slippery the banks are, and how fiercely the current flows—can all be interpreted as indicators of how hard the transformation will be.

To dream of a placid lake or a pond is another aquatic indicator of happiness. Not unnaturally, an unruffled surface is deemed to forecast luck and good fellowship. To see a lake silvered by moonlight augurs well for a romantic encounter, in which you may enjoy the affection of someone you have long admired. A note of caution should be sounded, however, if you see yourself swimming or wading out of your depth. This should be taken as a warning to guard against promiscuity.

Salt Water

Rivers and lakes are destined to mingle their waters with the wide currents of the open ocean and in the symbolism of dreams the sea is seen to stand for the strength of the emotions. The all-enveloping nature of sea water is enough to balance the power of the psyche. When considering how dreams of the sea might be interpreted, it is important to distinguish between the shallows of the shoreline, which equate to the superficial, and deeper offshore waters, which carry the notation of brevity and depth. Menaced in dreams by high seas, the term "stormy waters" offers far less encouragement to the sleeper than the security of shoal-water and the tide-line.

Even the comparative safety of the shore may hold dangers. A classic obstacles dream involves trying to swim

ashore on a rocky coastline over which crashing ocean breakers pound the shore. The imagery stands for a difficult decision or action that has to be faced. This is the unconscious mind's method of appealing to the dreamer not to be defeated by what might at first glance appear to be the insurmountable task of reaching safety.

A common dream involving the sea is that of a small island, usually perceived as a traditional desert island, fringed with tropical palm trees and golden sands. Its idyllic appearance may, however, indicate your present state of boredom, where despite comfortable surroundings very little happens, or is likely to happen. Indeed, even a walk along the island's beach may prove urksome. Wet sand against the dreamer's skin or its scratching within clothing may prove an irritant, warning against complacency, much as a medieval monk's hair-shirt was a constant rejoinder to guard against worldly distraction.

Until a few decades ago, instances of underwater dreams were usually restricted to the claustrophobic sensations of drowning, but thanks to wildlife documentaries and the increased popularity of scuba-diving, the undersea world has blossomed into a rich source of dream imagery. Habitats, such as a coral reef are seen to be so unlike our own world that to visit them in dreams is to escape to a constantly changing kaleidoscope of form and ever-changing color. The sensation of floating weightlessly in this sensually intriguing environment can be likened to flying, where the sleeper is beguiled into forgetting the storm tossed waters that foam and boil overhead.

Weather Dreams and
Elemental Forces

In our dreams the sleeping mind uses aspects of nature that we encounter on a daily basis to impart the mundane. But to highlight the important, and to ensure we remember, the psyche may shock us with unsettling images of nature unleashed such as volcanoes, earthquakes, avalanches, or floods. Natural disasters such as these were thought to occur when the elemental forces of water, air, fire, and earth were out of balance with each other. The four elements are also regarded as potent symbols within dreamlore.

Calm and Storm

Any sensation of wind in a dream symbolizes energy and transformation and usually as the omens become worse, the greater the wind's force becomes. If serenity and calm pervade your dreamscape with nothing more than a gentle breeze to disturb the scene, it should be regarded as a sign of good fortune as it denotes a time of travail has passed, and a period of tranquillity is now about to take place in your life. The dreamer may, with practice, be able to envision a calm scene (perhaps a familiar or favorite place) and turn a disconcerting dream into one with a softer and more tranquil aspect.

If a light wind ruffles your dreamscape, it indicates a good time to start a new relationship, or launch a business venture. However, strong gusts of wind signal an unsettling period of frustration or symbolize the need to face up to a crisis. As in real life, to imagine an approaching storm is a sure sign that trouble lurks just around the corner, and you should remain cautious for a few weeks after the dream.

Hurricanes lie at the extreme limit of the Beauford scale, and to experience the frightful forces unleashed by its power is one of the most traumatic experiences nature can (quite literally)

throw at you. To dream of the ferocity of such an event may reflect severe anxiety about some forthcoming event in waking life. Perhaps it underlines the dreamers unease about a high risk venture, a move away from home, or concern about an inappropriate but passionate encounter. Either way, the psyche is graphically displaying its disquiet with powerful force.

Precipitation

Although it may be inconvenient to be caught in a downpour to dream of falling rain has long been considered a fortunate omen. A gentle shower symbolizes blessings descending and the grace of heaven being visited upon the land. In a dreamscape, rain is often regarded as the tears of the spirit, which flow to wash away grief and fear and to see it fall while the sun shines predicts that whatever problems you may currently have, will soon be swept away by the dawning of more fortuitous times.

To our ancestors the union of sun and rain, the rainbow, signified the presence of a benign deity. Because it was seen to span the heavens and earth, the rainbow became a particularly beneficent symbol linking mankind with the divine. Little wonder, therefore, that in dreamlore the rainbow has come to be regarded as an exceedingly fortuitous omen. To dream of a rainbow denotes travel and unexpected good news relayed to you by a stranger. For lovers it predicts a long and happy union. However, the rainbow's legendary "crock of gold" may prove illusory to those who seek easy money. The rainbow's true treasure is in its beauty and not in any fiscal reward.

To dream about being lost in a fog or mists in an eerie vision is usually taken as a cry for help, concerning a problem in the sleeper's life that is becoming obscured by irrelevances. To imagine emerging from the fog before waking promises a successful conclusion to the difficulties. Dreams of swirling mists, in which a familiar landscape appears drowned in a wash of confusion, may be your psyche highlighting unseen dangers that the dreamer should identify and so avoid stumbling over.

If frost and ice appear in your dream, it suggests a change may be beneficial in some area of your life. Ice symbolizes coldness, rigidity, and sterility, and your psyche may be urging you to display more emotional warmth in your dealings with those around you.

If rime and frost transform your dreamscape into a strangely magical land of sunlight and sparkle, the vision presented portends a visit to an exotic location that, hitherto, you know little about. However, to dream of an overnight frost, that destroys crops you

into a landscape alien to the senses, It is beguiling to the eye with glint and dazzle, muffles sound, and numbs the sense of touch. Its sudden appearance in a dream denotes a new beginning, but one that must be acted upon quickly, or the chance may fade away. A persistent omen (according to old almanacs) suggests that to dream of falling snowflakes may cause a lover's tiff. Eating snow is considered to forebode poverty, whereas imagining slush or dirty snow forebodes humbled pride. You will have to seek reconciliation with a person you previously held in contempt.

The Elements

To the ancient philosophers, water, fire, earth, and air represented the four elements that sustained the world, and from which all other matter was composed. They were thought to permeate everything—both the living and the inanimate. Each of the elements was seen as a vital component of the flesh and spirit of humanity and its wellbeing was a matter of keeping a balance between the four. Water, fire, air, and earth each evolved their specific symbolism and dreamlore interpretation.

have planted, cautions the dreamer to avoid claiming success until it has truly been earned. Frozen ponds or lakes offer a further warning: to beware promises, which like the ice are easily broken.

Snow has long been regarded as a symbol of purity and beauty, transforming our world of the familiar

full of glint and dazzle, offers the prospect of a lively and effervescent encounter, but dreaming of deep, still water carries the caution to beware those of few words, the silent type, whose calm persona may hide malignant thoughts. Be forewarned by the old proverb, "in a pack, it is seldom the barking dog that bites."

To see a reflection in water symbolizes the transient nature of life, where the merest breeze can ruffle the waters and so the vision is lost. The imagery serves to caution against putting your faith in unworthy friends. If the elements of water and air are brought into conflict, strong winds create waves, and the symbolism evoked represents human emotion with their ebb and flow, rage or calm. To dream of high waves at sea is an omen of short-lived friendships, whereas waves on a lake indicate intolerance. Struggling against mighty forces during your sleep indicates a forceful and obstinate character which (depending upon the circumstance) could either be your main asset, or it can lead to your downfall.

The Element of Water

Water is a common theme in dreams and its connection with the uterine fluid of the womb and its role in evolution make it a symbol of emergent life and rebirth. There are folktales of healing waters in most cultures, and in dreams, as in baptism, to be immersed in water is to be spiritually cleansed.

Water is generally regarded as a fortunate omen, and to dream of drawing water either from a tap or well, denotes favorable prospects in fortune and love. However, to spill the water denotes a quarrel. Fast flowing water,

The Element of Fire

Fire is considered the most fearsome and consuming of the four dream elements and symbolizes the passion of the emotions and the scourging power of flame. To frequently dream of fire indicates an excitable temperament that would benefit from a greater degree of self-control and temperance.

In mythology, Prometheus stole fire from the gods—the sacred flame of wisdom that divided the world of men from the divinity of heaven—and brought it to earth. Thereafter, fire assumed a contradictory meaning. It can burn and destroy, or cleanse and purify. The key to its omen is the impression of being burnt. If the emphasis of the dream is more on light shed, than upon heat radiated, it should be seen as a good omen. However, to be scorched by flames presages the suggestion of redemption through ordeal.

During illness, you may dream of trying to subdue a fire that has been raging out of control. This should be regarded as a talisman to indicate you are on the way to recovery. Similarly, to be encircled by flame, foretells the sleeper has a creative, inventive, or artistic nature that they know little about, but yearns for outlet and expression.

The Element of Air

By its nature we rarely see air in dreams, but its importance as one of the elements is illustrated by what it supports. Air upholds weather systems, it is the spiritual medium for flight and (most importantly) it is the very "breath of life." Eastern philosophies believe that the body's vital energies are carried in air and Aristotle speculated that a fifth element, the quintessence, was transferred to all living things through the air. Little wonder, therefore, that writers on dreamlore have included entries about it since earliest times. One famous sixteenth-century source, *The Dream of Joseph*, declared that "to see air clear and fair makes promise of success

to all persons; but to see air misty, dark or cloudy portends the hindrance of action."

To dream of breathing warm air denotes the possible onset of an illness or coming under an evil influence, while the feeling of cold air foretells a courageous disposition that resists temptation and will not easily be put aside. Feeling stifled in a dream by stale air or oppressive humidity indicates an ill-advised friendship or union that the dreamer would be well advised to terminate.

Air's elemental domain is the sky and in dreams it is the appearance of the firmament that govern the omens. Serene clear blue skies (the clearer the better) offer the prospect of a respite from life's worries, whereas the old adage about storm clouds gathering forebode an unsettled period of

hardship for the sleeper. A grey blanket of cloud that obscures the horizon indicates the dreamer may be creating a bad impression among those they can least afford to alienate. Heavy, rain-laden clouds portend further problems, indicating a period of vexation, but one you will eventually triumph over.

The Element of Earth

Of all the elements, three are sacred to the gods, but the fourth, earth, is purely the domain of humanity. It is the most basic of the elemental forces and in

dreams invariably symbolizes the solid and practical side of our nature. If you imagine yourself digging in the earth it should be interpreted as a sign of future prosperity, both physically and spiritually. Sandy soil denotes uncertainties; red earth symbolizes hard work and toil; and rich, dark soil portends satisfaction and contentment. Parched earth, however, is seen as a sign of evil intent, where its barren nature reflects inner conflict. You should search your dreamscape for signs of hope, such as emergent growth or the first spots of rain.

Mud, as the union of two elemental forces, is believed in many religions to symbolize creation. It specifically means the creation of mankind. In biblical lore God molded Adam from a lump of clay and breathed life into him and traditionally it is to clay and dry-boned dust that man returns. Early sources claimed that to dream about mud foretold finding hidden riches, particularly gold and silver, while a dream in which you sank into mud led to a rapid recovery of health after a long illness.

Stones were also worshiped in the past or used as a conduit between heaven and earth. At Stonehenge, great standing stones combine with the powerful symbolism of the circle to form a megalithic temple that still, after four thousand years, defies a rational answer to its precise purpose. To dream of standing stones or a granite obelisk (used in Egyptian sun worship) may be evoked by distant echoes from an ancestral past. It is a dream to cherish as it builds bridges between you and a long-vanished age.

Natural Disasters

When nature pushes the elements to extremes, portentous events ensue. Volcanoes and lightning summons fire; an unstable Earth unleashes quakes and avalanches; water creates floods and drought; and air stirs hurricanes and typhoons into angry motion. It is little wonder, therefore, that the dreamer chooses to employ the symbolism of catastrophe and disaster to give import to the world of the sleeping mind.

The earliest oracles linked dreams about volcanoes with the passion of

love, albeit based on deceit. An eighteenth-century almanac declared that a woman who dreamed of an active volcano would be driven by greed and selfishness to "ensnare a husband by wantonly flaunting her charms." In dreamlore today volcanoes are seen to represent carnal desire, wherein strong emotions may be held in check, yet bubble away just below the surface to be released in a violent eruption of pent-up fury. Hot passions are aroused, and care should be taken lest desire turn into dangerous obsession.

The power to bring down fire from the heavens in the form of lightning bolts has long been considered the prerogative of the gods. Native Americans associate the phenomenon with the universal spirit—the Thunderbird—and in many cultures the zigzag shape of the lightning flash symbolizes the ability to cross the bridge between worlds. In a dream, to be struck by a thunderbolt implies intuition, inspiration, and the awakening realization that you possess psychic powers.

If earthquakes or avalanches disturb your dream, the omens are not encouraging. The former have been a feature of sleep since antiquity, when earthquakes supposedly foretold war and turmoil. Today the dream is interpreted as indicating upheaval and a change of environment. To dream of an

avalanche denotes formidable problems, which haunt the sleeper's mind and continue to build up in their waking life. These troubles require a fresh appraisal or a completely different approach to problem solving.

The disasters of flood and drought portend hardship for the dreamer, yet both offer a degree of solace. To dream that you are menaced by rising water, or that your house is flooded, indicates that a personal crisis may lie in wait.

However, if adequate precautions are put into place, there is nothing that cannot be overcome by determination. Similarly, a dream in which you endure a drought portends misfortune. Work will prove a drudge for scant reward; but the dreamer can take comfort that this harrowing time will pass, leaving you wiser and better prepared for any future pitfalls that fate may choose to lay across your path.

The Earth's Riches

Lying within the earth, encased in rock fissures, are incredible treasures, which mankind has coveted and dreamed about since the dawn of civilization. The world's currencies have revolved around them for nearly three thousand years; ever since King Croesus of Lydia struck the first pure gold coins.

Gold and Silver

Stone Age men were attracted by shining specks in river gravel, which they discovered were pliable, and could be hammered into ornaments. What these early civilizations did not realize, however, was that their crude workmanship bore the stamp of eternity. Gold is impervious to the ravages of the centuries and can be melted down time and again without shedding any of its qualities. A single ounce can be drawn out to make an unbroken thread 35 miles long, or hammered into a leaf less than a millionth of an inch thick.

In most Eastern and Western traditions, gold and silver were considered to be the solidification of solar and lunar energy. Gold's association with the mystical aspect of the sun make the metal a symbol of divine illumination, purity, and immortality.

In dreamlore, to imagine gold in your sleep indicates honor and recognition or success in a current enterprise. It may forecast great wealth, but as with most dreams of sudden affluence, it carries the caution against placing too much reliance upon money to the detriment of personal relationships and health.

Silver, as a metal associated with the moon, has come to represent feminine spirituality: "the sun is king, the moon, queen." It symbolizes chastity and eloquence (hence silver tongued) but has acquired ambivalence within Christian tradition, where Judas betrayed Christ for thirty pieces of silver. To dream of this metal is never a comforting omen and is generally taken to warn against shortcomings in others such as the falsehood of friends and the deceit of acquaintances.

Decorative and Working Metals

The need to hew raw materials from the earth has existed since prehistoric man first dug the ground in search of flint for tool making. Unlike fortunate finds of precious metal, a dream in which quarries or mines appear demonstrates a commitment of time and effort toward achieving a goal. To see yourself working in a mine or quarry suggests that your present low fortunes will soon be raised by your own hard work and determination to succeed. However, to imagine mining gold or silver foretells ambitions that remain tantalizingly out of reach.

Dreams of metal generally infer that the sleeper shares some of its cold, hard qualities and would benefit from a more relaxed attitude when dealing with those around them. Individual metals each have their own omens. A dream in which brass appears denotes great physical and emotional strength, but if the metal is seen to be tarnished a period of introspection or a minor crisis may be indicated. Copper objects signify ungrounded fears and worries, or may represent the solution to a problem that has vexed you for some considerable time. Verdigris on the metal (a chemical reaction between copper and the atmosphere) is indicative of an apparent change for the better that may have been urged upon the sleeper. However, the green appearance of the verdigris points to duplicity and it is likely that only a token improvement has actually taken place. Another metal of suspicious omen, lead, is said to deliver contagion upon those who dream of it and to imagine lead in its molten form foretells that, by impatience, you will bring failure on your own hopes and upon the aspirations of others.

The first iron known to man was in the form of meteors, whose spectacular arrival appeared to make them gifts from the gods. When man learned to dig for iron and forge the metal, it revolutionized the making of tools and the casting of weapons. Such was its repute that in folklore iron assumed an almost magical status and was regarded as a powerful talisman. A prime example was the horseshoe used to ward off malevolent spirits. Among the worthy qualities associated with iron in dreams is an ability to indicate periods of substantial and energetic growth in either financial or romantic matters.

However, to envisage rust upon the metal reverses the omen and so the dreamer should prepare for disappointment, as events will conspire to snatch success from their grasp.

Gems, Crystals, and Precious Stones

Gemstones are the mineral products of earth's enormous pressures and temperatures with names that are hallmarks of beauty: amethyst, emerald, topaz, sapphire, ruby, opal, diamond, and lapis lazuli. All arouse man's admiration for their splendor, but also his avarice for their worth. This duel nature is reflected in the Christian myth that gemstones were created when Lucifer

fell to earth from heaven, and his angelic light shattered into millions of lustrous fragments.

Of all the precious stones, the diamond is the hardest. Its name is a corruption of adamant, so called because the diamond cuts all other natural substances, and can only be polished by one of its own kind. The jewel symbolizes permanence and incorruptibility, and owning one is a propitious dream. Its possession signifies the sleeper will receive recognition and high honor in their chosen profession or career.

Rubies were once considered a sure remedy for plague and an antidote to poison so they were greedily sought by medieval royalty, who had good reason to fear both fates. In dreamlore its glowing red heart symbolizes raw passion and may indicate indifference toward your partner and the desire for more amorous encounters. Sapphires, on the other hand, were seen to embody the blue coloration of the heavens and the heavenly virtues of truth and chastity. In dreams they warn against impulsive behavior and the false flattery of those who would try to beguile you.

The symbolic ambivalence of gemstones is exemplified by the belief that emeralds were formed from the saliva from serpents' fangs and is seen to represent both venomous hatred and spiritual wisdom. The poisonous aspect of the emerald denotes the inherent evil of material possessions (the stone carries its traditional bad luck into dreams), while the emerald, as an amulet, urges the dreamer to search their own soul for the inherent goodness therein.

Semi-precious stones and crystals also have rich symbolic association. To see the violet-blue glint of amethyst in your dreamscape cautions against the perils of intoxication; topaz denotes that you may bring misfortune upon yourself due to a fiery temper; while to imagine the iridescent flash of opals, signals a path through life lit by bright prospects.

In the ancient civilizations of Mesopotamia, lapis lazuli symbolized the firmament and the rich blue stone was used to decorate temple ceilings. In dreamlore it has come to represent talent that, if unchecked, will soar forever skyward, until it disappears from view—an omen of caution, not to let your special gifts blind you to the realities of everyday life. Dreams in which agate feature sometimes have undercurrents of sorrow and foretell that sympathy may shortly be expressed toward the sleeper. Jade is a more encouraging stone to dream about as its omens are invariably progressive. The Chinese believed the purest form of jade (the rare apple-green variety) conferred the power of levitation upon its owner, but modern analysis link the dream's interpretation to completing a difficult task involving much serious contemplation and the success of the intellect after lengthy striving.

Organic Riches

The semi-precious materials in this section owe their origins, not to the geological forces that have shaped our planet, but to the action of living organisms. A prime example of this organic growth is the relationship between the oyster and the pearl. In dreamlore it is seen as a metaphor, illustrating how beauty can be brought forth from ugliness. Their origins in the depths of the sea implies hidden knowledge and esoteric wisdom and the translucent hue and moon-like shimmer of pearls allow them to stand

for tears of joy and of sorrow. The purity of the pearl also diametrically opposes the symbolism of the oyster, which has come to be regarded in dreamlore as a forceful symbol of sexuality. One source states "to imagine prizing apart the shell of the oyster to expose its inner flesh is a desire for seduction, regardless of consequence!"

Just as a pearl is the protective mechanism employed by an oyster against the intrusion and irritation of a grain of sand, so is amber the consequence of an injured tree's action to guard itself against the risk of infection. Dreams of finding this fossilized resin on the tide line of a beach, invariably offer optimistic

explanations, denoting that a state of balance and harmony exist within the sleeper's psyche.

Coral also offers a favorable portent for the future, but dreams of a coral reef signal danger for anyone with money and unrealistic ideas.

Ivory was prized as gold and as a result of its color and hardness was considered to be a gem. Unlike silver and gold that could be resmelted, or jewels that could be recut, once ivory is carved it remained unchangeable. This permanence was reflected in the world of dreams, where ivory was thought to denote wisdom and longevity. A curious fantasy, related by Sir Thomas Browne in the seventeenth century, stated that our dreams passed through either a gate wrought of ivory, or one made of horn. The dream that passed through the gate of ivory was delusional, whereas those that passed the gate of horn came true. The barbarity of obtaining ivory and the contempt in which the trade is currently held mean that outmoded symbolism relating to dreams involving ivory can no longer be trusted. Indeed, after four hundred years Browne's ivory gate really does prove delusional.

Adornment and Treasure

Humanity's self-aggrandisement and desire for ostentatious display manifests itself in the wearing of jewelry. We have called upon the earth's riches to create works of art that range in diversity from the earliest Neolithic brass bangles, to the majesty of royal regalia.

The Romans were the first to record the symbolism of jewelry in dreams, which they prophesied to be an omen of good fortune, so long as it was given or received, but never bought. To imagine wearing an ostentatious display of jewels was seen as a rebuke to guard against self-flattery and falling victim to impulsive behavior. Current interpretation suggests that the importance of a dream about jewelry depends upon whether it is lost or stolen and, ultimately, if the item is recovered before waking.

Gems and jewels lend added sparkle to the world of sleep, and to dream of a necklace foretells the accumulation of wealth. But if it should break, the provenance will disappear "like water through a sieve." For a woman to dream that she is wearing a bracelet indicates gossip and slander, while to allow a partner to fasten one on her indicates

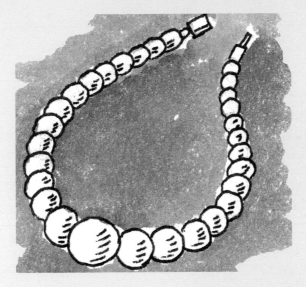

she will be dominated by that person. Earrings were traditionally worn by sailors as a talisman against the threat of drowning at sea—a fate made more likely by the fact that few sailors bothered to learn how to swim. To dream of wearing an earring was once considered to forebode a quarrel between sweethearts. However its modern equivalent is likely to represent the psyche's dalliance with the dreamer's own sexuality.

A common theme within the realm of dreams is to imagine finding treasure or uncovering buried riches. The hoard is traditionally seen to consist of gold, silver, and precious stones. The treasure may be guarded by a dragon or serpent, spiritual deities summoned up by our unconscious mind to underline the importance of the riches we have so fortuitously uncovered. The treasure, however, is unlikely to represent wealth, but symbolizes instead whatever is most worthwhile to the dreamer, such as love or spiritual values or perhaps even life itself.

The Body

We each know our own body better than anything else and it comes as no surprise that sleepers find it frequently occurring in dreams. Our dreams are preoccupied with our daily mechanisms, the senses, and how we use or abuse our body.

Pregnancy and Birth

Sometimes dream symbolism can be interpreted in a literal way. If you dream that you, or your partner, are pregnant, it could simply be wish fulfilment, and if this is a desirable outcome the dream may even prove to be prophetic. Alternatively, pregnancy can be seen to represent creativity and new beginnings. You may be nurturing an idea for a project that needs your commitment to move it forward.

Rather surprisingly, male pregnancy is a dream that many men will experience at some time during their life. Obviously we need to look at the dream in broader and more symbolic terms. Analysis suggests a need to reconnect with the "child within" and take a more simplistic approach to life. The dreamer needs to find joys and wonderment wherever they can be found. New life, signified by pregnancy, is similar to dreams of life after death and indicates a desire to transcend human existence and discover your true self. The foetus is that element of your psyche that may have been overlooked,

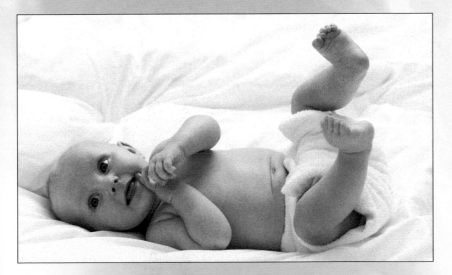

but now seeks rediscovery and encouragement. Dreams about birth are generally taken to be positive omens, indicating both financial and physical well-being. If the labor is perceived to be difficult, it denotes there are problems to overcome and decisions that must be addressed. Your practical, rational mind will, however, resolve these issues in your favor.

The symbol of a baby in a dream may simply reflect a wish to nurture an actual infant, but is more commonly interpreted to stand as a symbol of self and a desire to return to a less complicated age, when the sleeper was indulged and had their every need taken care of. Although the dreamer might feel exhausted due to repeated failure, by envisaging themselves as a baby they are able to recreate a time of supreme contentment. Dreams of infants suckling milk may further underline our desire to escape the realities of life, and these earliest of our memories can be among the happiest and most carefree images that our subconscious employs.

The Face

Our face is the object we are most familiar with. It smiles or frowns back at us with each glance in the mirror and upon it is written our past history, etched into each line and contour. It is how we imagine others to perceive us, and in dreamlore represents intellect and logic. To envisage your own head or face in a dream foreshadows a period of introspection and self-examination. It shows a need to ensure that your mental welfare is all that it should be. To view the face of a friend or relative (particularly if they are deceased) may herald a message. Try to imagine the context in which they might appear to you and then deduce from their demeanor whether the message bodes well. A smiling countenance portends good luck, but a sad or angry demeanor may be intended as a reproach or a guilty secret that the sleeper chooses to hide behind or ignore.

To dream of the eye reflects the importance placed upon the sense of sight in the waking world. Many omens have been attributed to eyes, "the windows of the soul," and in past times their color was thought to represent specific qualities or failings. Blue eyes

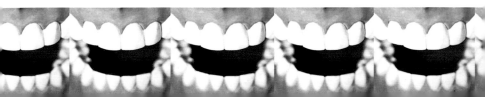

denoted beauty weakened by inconsistency; gray and hazel eyes suggested a love of flattery; while brown eyes cautioned against guile and deceit.

The eye has long been regarded as a sacred symbol and when it is seen within a pyramid (as on American dollar bills) it represents the all-seeing power of God. Its potency as a talisman has echoes in dreamlore, where to see a pair of beautiful, smiling eyes is considered a precursor to love and contentment. However, an injury to the eye should be taken as a warning to act cautiously in business dealings and to ensure that all transactions are visibly beyond reproach.

Dreams concerned with ears and the mouth may reflect the dreamer's concern that they are being talked about behind their back. To imagine that other people are spreading gossip reflects the common concern that, in waking life, you are undervalued and overlooked. Alternatively, to dream of an ear or a whispering mouth might signify that the dreamer will soon hear some exciting news.

To imagine an open mouth in a dream usually signifies trouble such as an argument or an ongoing quarrel, where neither side has the good grace to make concessions. To see a laughing mouth is likely to portend a period of reckless behaviour, whereas dreaming of a pair of full, sensual lips is indicative of a person whose mood swings erratically between extremes. For women, dreams of applying lipstick have powerful sexual overtones and can be viewed as demonstrating a desire for sexual encounter and adventure.

Anxiety regarding an impending dental appointment may prompt a dream about teeth, but if no treatment is scheduled, a dream concerning tooth decay or one in which your teeth fall out, is likely to indicate your fear of losing your health, your looks, or even your potency. In essence, teeth (or the lack of them) focus attention upon the dreamer's concern of growing old.

The Body's Core

Dreams in which the neck feature are invariably concerned with balance. It is perceived to have a pivotal role in dreamlore connecting the head, the domain of the intellect, with that of the body, where sensuality and sexuality hold sway. Thus, the neck is regarded as both a bridge and a barrier, between the forces of impetuosity and reasoned restraint. A dream in which you may be said to be "up to your neck in trouble" is the subconscious mind's way of warning the dreamer to beware the trap of letting your heart rule your head. It is a warning not to take unnecessary risks for short-term gratification.

If the shoulders or back play a role in your dream, it is likely to represent a caution to take guard against double-dealing and deceit. In waking life we are unlikely to view our own back (save with difficulty, by straining round to glimpse it in a mirror) so it is largely unchartered territory, and has long been regarded with suspicion. The dreamer who sees a naked back may feel ambivalent toward its owner, yet to have a person literally turn their back on you is a sign that you are afraid of alienation, and will do almost anything to prevent the emptiness of rejection.

To dream of a man with a broad chest signifies strength and prosperity. A woman similarly endowed has been considered a portent since the time of the Ancient Greeks—the larger the breasts, the more favourable the omen! Despite its sexual connotations, this area of a woman's body is not considered to occupy a particularly significant role in male dreamscapes. Upon waking, men are far more likely to report dreams of lingerie or swimwear than fully exposed breasts. It would appear that, in dreams at least, there is delight to be had in the understated and the concealed.

Arms and Legs

To dream of either an arm or a leg, and in particular to see yourself the possessor of strong muscular limbs, signifies that the sleeper will achieve their goal in life by hard work and patient toil. Alternatively, it may indicate a restoration to health after an illness or operation. Withered or amputated limbs reverse the omen, while to dream that you break an elbow or wrist foretells a personality that is easily bent to the will of others.

Hands and fingers are capable of a grace that convey messages with an elegance that speech can seldom match. How the dreamer holds or positions their hands is likely to reflect conflicts in waking life. Loose, free flowing gestures indicate contentment, while tightly held fists or screwed up fingers, speak of current emotional problems clouding the sleeper's horizon.

To dream of a child's hand can indicate financial gain and to imagine that a baby grips your fingers represents purity and a future possibility of a birth. This is not necessarily that of a child, it could represent the birth of a cherished idea or project that is destined to reach maturity. Dirty or bloodied hands suggest future problems and washing them symbolizes a need to rectify a misdemeanor, or be rid of a past embarrassment. If these imply a guilty conscience the dream might well be

accompanied by an accusatory and pointing finger.

In dreamlore, legs and feet are seen as the basis for stability in life. They are our bedrock and frequently symbolize a desire to find our feet and to make the very best of whatever opportunities fate presents. Not unsurprisingly, dreams involving injured legs are symbolic of poverty and to become lame suggests a gradual decline of fortune and favor. A grazed or swollen knee in a dream warns us to use money wisely, whereas to see a bandaged leg or foot cautions the sleeper against being beguiled by flattery, lest their money and their good name be stolen away.

Enter Within

What covers the body surface and what is beneath are symbols commonly employed by the subconscious mind to enliven our dreams. The largest of the human organs, the skin, is symbolic of the power of touch and erotic pleasure. Through utilizing its imagery, the dreamer is made aware of their own sexuality, and the need to shed some inhibitions. Perhaps they are regarded as puritanical and would benefit from displaying more emotional warmth.

If the human body is considered to house a soul, then the heart is seen in dreamlore to symbolize its sincerity and compassion. It represents the center, the literal "heart of our being." To envisage that you dream of a heart is one of the most encouraging omens and is frequently associated with true love and romance. However, to dream of your own heart (living and beating within your chest) foretells weakness and a lack of energy.

To dream that you suffer a heart attack is seldom prophetic, yet it may represent a jolt (albeit unpleasant and alarmist) from your subconscious to encourage you to amend bad habits. Perhaps you should consider a healthier diet, or try cutting back on nicotine, alcohol, or any other of the crutches that we may lean upon to the detriment of our well-being.

Blood is symbolic of our life-force, and in some religions is held to be sacred. Little wonder, therefore, that dreams in which blood is shed are held to bode ill, and may possibly indicate health worries.

To bleed in a dream is seen to deplete the sleeper of their spiritual force. It could possibly show that the burden of worrying about a friend or relative has drained the person of their psychic energy. Any dream in which you shed blood may be taken to indicate that you fear the loss of your strength. You should therefore beware of colleagues or work rivals, who may take advantage of that weakness. For adolescent girls, the symbolism of blood stands for menstruation and the rites of passage from child to womanhood.

Bone and muscle represent the structure and dynamism of the body. Dreams of the latter symbolize strength in men yet predict a life of toil and hardship when envisioned by a woman. Muscles imply a struggle against rivals, whether on the sportsfield, or on the floor of the office. If the dreamer can visualize themselves winning, such conflicts can actually empower them in working life.

When bones are envisioned in a dream it demonstrates that the sleeper has a relaxed attitude to their own mortality. Nothing more ably demonstrates this than the dream image of a skull, the "shell of death," which lies a mere skin's depth away from each and every one of us. Its appearance serves to remind the dreamer that, by agonizing over small details and shallow options, they may lose sight of the bigger picture.

Traces of Self

The shadow and footprint appear in dreamlore as an insubstantial witness to our presence. It is formed by us, but not of us. In Jungian terms, the shadow is interpreted as the repressed or unacknowledged part of ourselves. Ancient wisdom viewed the shadow with suspicion, as it was that part of man that interrupted the flow of light from heaven to earth. Because of this, it was seen as an omen that offered little comfort and suggested the dreamer would bring shame upon themselves.

To see your own footprints in a dream foretells a route or strategy that will guide you to victory over a rival, achieved by your own unbending personality. To imagine that you see footprints in sand or snow foretells a period of indecision and inner conflict; whereas to follow in another's footsteps quite logically denotes a lack of drive and ambition.

Images of Self

The symbolism of the mirror is often selected by the subconscious to reflect how we perceive ourselves and how we believe (or would like to believe) others see us. However, dreamlore cautions against the sin of vanity and has engrained within the mirror a patina of mistrust, no doubt enhanced by the story of Narcissus who drowned while admiring his own reflection. As a general rule, reflected images are to be considered false and so interpret a mirror dream by reversing its apparent message.

Perceptions and delusions of self-beauty or ugliness are strangely juxtaposed within the dreamscape. To imagine that you receive a proposal of marriage from an ugly partner portends that you will wed an attractive person. Similarly, for a woman to dream that she is beautiful, or for a man to imagine himself excessively handsome, may be taken as a caution to guard against the conceit of pride. Self-flattery carries a contrary message. Those who consider themselves to be perfect are unwittingly, yet invariably, destined for the greatest fall.

Images of self-insecurity are widely reported by dreamers and research suggests that two situations appear most often. The first is the act of undressing in public and the second casts the dreamer naked into a totally inappropriate setting. Each scenario plays upon our deepest insecurities, yet the subconscious mind may not be setting out to be deliberately cruel, rather it seeks to confront your vulnerability and by revealing all help the dreamer to unburden the repressive detritus that may have accumulated over the years.

The dreamer may be unduly shy, or feel ashamed of their body; possibly as a result of a casual reprimand for some minor indiscretion. The dream seeks to expunge the stain by dismissing their nudity as irrelevant.

Worries

Our mind may deliberately exaggerate the image we have of ourselves. In dreams the question, "am I too fat?" or "am I too thin?" may continually reoccur to highlight the need of the sleeper to reconsider the way in which they use or abuse their body. In dreams you may appear grotesquely overweight, or ridiculously thin, and although deliberately exaggerated by the psyche, it would be wise to heed the underlying message and to act upon its prompting. There are few people who would not benefit from a little self-improvement.

Our body's small imperfections also fall prey to our dreaming mind, which chooses to highlight our insecurities by introducing images such as freckles, spots, and blemishes to reflect the unease we may feel about our appearance. This exaggeration (usually blown-up out of all proportion) serves merely to denote our trifling worries over nothing.

Hair is another important factor in our image of self and dreaming about having long, flowing hair is taken as a sign of good health. Short hair indicates an enthusiastic desire to "push-on and finish the job." An unsuitable (or even ludicrous) haircut, or hairstyle, encountered in the realms of sleep, implies that you fear a rival for the attention of someone you hold dear and to dream of suddenly changing your hair color (particularly for men) is a subconscious warning to guard against the deceitful actions of those you have professional contact with.

Not unsurprisingly, signs of aging impertinently intrude themselves into our dreams to remind the sleeper that, although we would wish it otherwise, the passage of time will eventually outflank us. The subconscious mind gently reminds us of our own mortality in dreams that might typically include such images as graying hair, sudden baldness, or wrinkles. Despite the latter's current unpopularity (and the zealous attention of the surgeon's syringe and scalpel), wrinkles have long been regarded as a symbol of serenity and are taken to portend an eventful and prosperous life. Similarly, gray hair should be considered a welcome sight in the dreamscape as it denotes a sage wisdom, born of experience and maturity. To lose hair (often by the handful) may be an alarming theme to be presented within a dream, but its shock value serves merely to caution against the deceit of human vanity. You should learn to accept the inevitable gracefully, for it is the qualities that lie deep within yourself that reflect your true worth.

In Sickness and in Health

Concerns about health problems spill readily into our dreams. Just as in waking life, the dreamer may seem preoccupied with illness and disease, aging, or even death. These portents should not alarm the sleeper. They inevitably represent a coded warning that our psyche sends to instigate change. When symptoms appear to be really bad, it is often the case that the dream omens indicate the exact opposite in real life. However, as a general word of warning, if your health is giving you cause for concern always ensure that you receive qualified advice and the correct professional treatment is sought at the earliest opportunity.

Illness and Injury

A common dream is one in which the sleeper suffers injury or illness. However, the sensation of pain that should accompany the condition may seem strangely muted (in the case of serious illness) or deeply intensified (for a minor complaint). In these instances it is the pain itself, not the condition, that the psyche wants the sleeper to focus their attention upon. It may be a warning against taking unnecessary risks or an attempt by the subconscious to instigate a more beneficial approach toward life.

Dreams where your body seems fatigued or feels racked with pain (you might even jolt awake covered in sweat) may signify that in waking life you are needlessly worrying over problems that are not really your concern or are of little consequence. Take a more relaxed approach and do not let the best of life pass you by. Alternatively, the dream may warn you to stop seeking sympathy for supposed or invented troubles as perceived ills are often far harder to heal than actual ones.

Sometimes the subconscious mind will inflict a pain dream upon the sleeper almost as an act of revenge for some supposed misdemeanor in waking life. If you are on a diet and eat something you know to be strictly off-limits, your conscious (waking) mind might find a seemingly rational excuse for the action, but your psyche is not so easily deceived, and may punish and purge what it perceived to be slack behavior with images of illness or the sensation of pain.

Among the most disturbing of dreams are those involving accidents. Although the events foreseen may (in extremely rare cases) be a premonition of an actual event, it is far more likely that the omens seek to come to terms with the fact that accidents cannot always be prevented, and the unpleasant question must be addressed—"what might happen if ...?"

Perhaps one of the worse scenarios that can be imagined in an accident-dream is to be impaled. Gothic imagery appeals to the sleeping mind and impalement is a popularly reported topic in dreamlore. Whether a plausible slip from a roof onto railings below, or the fantasy of a "vampire-style" stake through the heart, the essence of the dream is the pain of unwanted intrusion. The omens may hint at fear of sexual penetration, but more frequently they warn the sleeper to be on the look out for threats from enemies. Only if the dreamer escapes before waking can they be assured of avoiding danger.

Losing Control

One of the events we all fear is losing control of our faculties. We fear the unexpected occurrence of blindness or deafness, the sudden onset of paralysis, or the mental turmoil of insanity. Such fears gnaw at our confident assumptions that life will progress smoothly as normal and instead we will be ambushed with problems of unexpected intensity.

To dream that you have suddenly become blind is widely chronicled in dreams and usually relates to an object that you eagerly seek, but because of your blindness are unlikely to find. The object is generally your hopes and goals in life, and becoming blind indicates that the dreamer has literally lost sight of their ambitions and is unclear about how to regain focus on them. To imagine being deaf in a dream, or unable to make contact with other people, may symbolize irresponsibility and laziness. The sleeper is indifferent to the mundane and needs to adopt a more realistic approach, otherwise all the small difficulties that you currently ignore, will suddenly swamp you.

Very often dreams of paralysis and numbness can simply be self-induced by the dreamer's arm or leg going to sleep as the result of a trapped nerve. Where this is not the case, however, dreams of being paralyzed or so numb that you are unable to move (as if rooted to the spot), seldom forewarn a

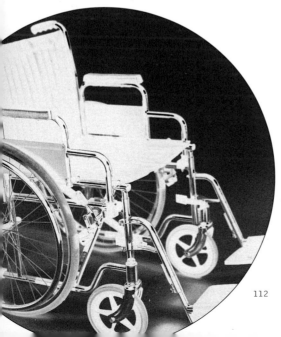

physical onset of the condition but stem from the sleeper's subconscious. The psyche may be equating paralysis with frigidity, where in waking life the dreamer fears sexual contact will expose some deep secret. Perhaps a man fears he is impotent, or a woman dreads comparison with previous lovers.

If you have dreams involving uncontrollable trembling fits or fever, they may appear far worse than the actual message they presage. To imagine you are stricken in this way, generally signifies that you worry unnecessarily over trifling affairs, or matters of no importance, while the best of life slips past unnoticed. You should try to cultivate more interests, perhaps by involving yourself with voluntary work to help the less fortunate.

To dream that you are insane, or your madness is so severe that even everyday tasks are completely impossible to perform, then the omens would appear less than auspicious. However, comfort may be taken from the fact that analytical thought requires a sound mind so, dreams of madness are exposed as dreams of contrary, where apparent symbolism is reversed. Usually such dreams reflect an unjustified humiliation from the past or a highly embarrassing moment that filters through to the psyche as unsettling images of lunacy.

Occasionally sleepers may experience a trembling or "wave" sensation when they awake. This may happen when quickly aroused from sleep (especially if it is deep sleep or involves a particularly lucid dream) and although disconcerting it is usually the result of momentary confusion between the sleeping and waking worlds, and should pass without concern. However, if this occurs on a regular basis, or if you feel dizzy or faint when you first rise (you may put it down to getting up too quickly) it would be prudent to seek medical advice as a problem with blood pressure could be indicated.

Care and Cure

If we are ill the first point of professional contact is usually with a doctor or a nurse, and to see either of

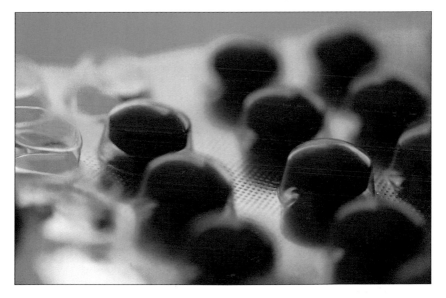

these in a dream is an encouraging omen. Doctors are among the most respected figures we deal with and, since they are a symbol of treatment and cure, to imagine a visit to their surgery augurs well for future health. Meeting a doctor in a social capacity indicates that friends will be happy to rally around and support you should you turn to them for help in a crisis. To see a nurse in a dream is also auspicious. If they look after children it indicates that you will enjoy a long and faithful relationship with your partner. To see a nurse leaving your house forebodes good health for the family, but to imagine you are nursed yourself indicates a maudlin temperament and you may well feel unwanted and vulnerable at the moment.

Dreams of visiting or being in a hospital always carry a note of apprehension. Most dreamers feel anxious and interpret the symbolism as a precognition dream, implying the sleeper, a member of their family, or a friend will face a traumatic period in hospital. Rest assured, this is seldom, if ever, the case. By envisioning a hospital, the dreamer may be expressing an element of personal phobia about illness. Thus, to imagine being hospitalized is a method the subconscious uses as a safety valve to release your innermost fears. If the dream is upsetting, it could indicate that you are under intolerable pressure, either at work or in your private life and need to talk things through with a sympathetic friend, who can help to unburden your load.

Dreams of medical matters and practitioners may also incorporate the symbolism of pills and medicine. To dream that you are given a dose of the latter is interpreted as a fortunate omen,

mcrops/9781856486699_P115I0.png

especially if it leaves a bitter taste in the mouth—the worse the better! The symbolism employs the twisted logic that anything that bad must be doing some good and implies that a person you once overlooked or disregarded will turn out to be a worthy asset as a friend. However, to dream that you are instructed to take pills reflects indecision and a timid nature. You are the only person who doubts your abilities, so try to instill more confidence and self-belief. Paradoxically, to administer tablets to another person in a dream portends causing pain to a close relative or friend.

Occasionally, the subconscious mind will choose a strange bedfellow for the dreamer, drawing on half-remembered tales from the past. One such image is that of the quack doctor, complete with snake oil and patient cure-alls. If such a suspicious character appears in your dreamscape, be warned of the possible treachery of strangers. A quack doctor further cautions against accepting new friends at face value. If you imagine resorting to patent medicines in a dream, it denotes you have a propensity to employ desperate measures to conquer a perceived idiosyncrasy in

your character. You have probably exaggerated the fault out of all proportion and are in danger of becoming obsessive.

Diagnosis and Recovery

The phobic alarm that hospitals engender has been discussed earlier, but a greater worry may be the actual examination and its diagnosis. These fears surface in dreamlore, where a favourable prognosis indicates you are secure and satisfied with the person you have become. However, diagnosing an illness points to the dreamer's insecurities and over-sensitive attitude to life. You need to find the renewed confidence to stop acting like one of

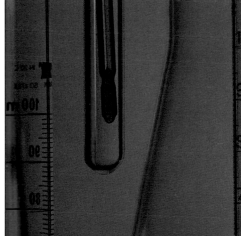

to take unnecessary risks with their health. A thermometer reveals a strong sense of responsibility and an inclination to get things done. The laboratory microscope has the power to reveal the smallest of organisms that if malicious or of evil intent could result in a life or death struggle for the host. In dreams the symbolism of the microscope begs the question: is the sleeper in danger of looking at things in too fine a detail and missing the bigger picture? Alternatively, they may read too much into just one aspect of a situation and miss its wider perspective.

Hypodermic syringes are one of the most disliked objects of dreamlore. We fear them for their menace of bodily intrusion and unlike a wasp, whose penetrating sting is over before we realize the event has happened, to be injected by a surgical syringe can seem like a drama played out in slow motion. However, as a dream symbol, the syringe (despite our exaggerated perceptions of pain) is a benign omen that works for our benefit and underlies the message that in life, small trials and

life's victims.

In the realm of dreams, the prospect of undergoing an operation is seldom to be relished. Its symbolism implies taking stock of life. Did you spend too much time at the office? Were you there when your family needed you? Have you achieved those childhood dreams? The omens tell you to get out and live your life—don't spend time brooding over past misfortune, don't be the one who never gets things done, and don't hold postmortems.

Medical instruments may well make an appearance in dreams about disease and diagnosis and to envision such specialist items as a scalpel or a stethoscope act to warn the sleeper not

tribulations are to be endured for the greater good.

If you are healthy and dream of recovering from an illness or operation, it indicates continued wellbeing; but to visualize the same circumstances when you are actually ill denotes a delay in your recovery. You should adopt a positive mental attitude and pay greater attention to fitness and diet, rather than simply expecting to get better without any effort.

Near-Death Experience

Over the past sixty years the concept of the near-death experience has been a controversial topic and has caused much scientific investigation and sceptical debate. However, despite the detractors (of whom there are many) the out-of-body-experience cannot always be explained away satisfactorily.

There are thousands of descriptions of near death experience given by men and women, who if anything were biased against accepting that such events happen. A common theme to the experience includes two distinct elements. The first is a feeling that the soul or spirit has left its earthly body and travels toward the radiant light of a better place. The writer Ernest Hemingway described it as "my soul... coming right out of my body, like you'd pull a silk handkerchief out of a pocket by one corner." The second element is the subsequent return to the body—rescued from death by medical treatment—and a sense of disappointment as the liberated spirit is pulled back into its earthly frame.

When near death has been experienced by those in life-threatening situations (such as major surgery or a severe accident) any further fear of death is assuaged by the conviction that their soul travels onward to a more serene environment. Great comfort can and should be taken from such visions.

Through the Gates

Mors janua vitae—Death, the Gate of Life—is how the Ancients envisaged the passage of the soul from life into death and on into mysteries far beyond their understanding. Mankind has been fascinated by the mystery of death ever since. The theme is a regular and recurring omen in dreamlore and is rarely (if ever) to be feared as a forecast of actual death or as a portent of evil.

Death may be compared to the last chapter of a book, where the turning of the final cover marks the closure of one particular way of being and the birth of something unimaginable and new. As a classic dream of contrary, a vision of death signifies a fresh start and new beginnings. Indeed, some dream almanacs go so far as to suggest the dreamer actually encourages a vision of death so that on waking life appears all the sweeter.

To dream of a corpse offers less encouragement and to see the dead body of a stranger cautions against entering into a partnership or ill-considered union. Give yourself time to reflect upon the idea and you will probably realize that your prospective partner differs from you so much that the relationship is doomed from the start. More ominously, to imagine you see your own corpse (the psyche's shock tactic at work again to jolt you into action) indicates your subconscious feels that you take too much from life and do not put enough back in. It suggests that through ministering to the needs of others, you will find contentment will be rebounding back upon yourself.

Last Rites of Passage

The death and burial of a loved one is always a highly charged event and it is little wonder that in the years or even decades that follow some of this emotional static will rub off into our dreams. One of the most foreboding images is that of the coffin and in the world of dreams the consensus of opinion suggests that it is another dream of contrary. Far from predicting a physical death, it signals that the sleeper has moved on from one particular period of their life to another. By

alluding to the uncompromising symbolism of a coffin, the psyche shows the dreamer that the change is irrevocable and the old order has gone. It is quite literally dead and buried.

Another of those strange dreams, where the omens completely contradict the implication, involve funerals. Most authorities agree that to witness a burial or cremation presages good fortune. A dream in which a funeral takes places is said to indicate an engagement, or a wedding; while to imagine your own funeral is a sign that a particularly difficult period in your life is about to come to a close. In a similar vein, to see an undertaker or to dream you do business with one is considered to promise a long and robust life. However, imagining that you are present at the reading of the deceased's will indicates your expectations of gain will rebound on you, and debts and insolvency may be forecast.

Tombs and Graves

Our mind's fascination with the mysterious and the macabre often focuses attention upon graves and tombs, and the paraphernalia that surround them. These are symbols of mortality and signposts to a land where we dare not tread.

The unsettling vision of your own grave in a dream signifies overwhelming difficulty and troubles that the dreamer fears they may never be able to dig their way out of. Neglected graves portend that a special project or secret ambition is doomed to failure; while to imagine you see a cracked or fallen tombstone may be a reminder from your subconscious mind never to take good health for granted, but to cherish it as your greatest asset.

A common nightmare reported to analysts is the sleeping vision of being buried alive. The horrors of going consciously to your grave are all too apparent, but it is possible that your discomfort is orchestrated by the psyche. It may be highlighting some dishonorable act from your past that you have not come to terms with and more importantly have not atoned for. Alternatively, the "burial" may suggest the need to move away from a bad influence, which is threatening to overwhelm the dreamer.

To imagine walking among the monuments in a church or cathedral is considered an omen of prosperity and to dream of a tomb, richly adorned with images symbolizing the earthly qualities of the deceased, indicates the impending arrival of favorable news.

However, if the sleeper dreams that they have their own coat of arms and can see it on a tomb or monument, it reflects a desire to rise above a perceived station in life and to enjoy a little of the cachet that being ennobled might bring. This reflects the desire to be accepted by those the sleeper incorrectly assumes to be their superiors.

Worship and Religion

Dreams play an important role in the Judaeo–Christian and Buddhist tradition and a large amount of their teaching is conveyed using symbolism and parables, much as the psyche delivers its messages to the sleeper. Symbolic language is the tongue of faith and these potent images are frequently assimilated into our dreamlore.

Visions of Heaven and Hell

Not unnaturally, dreams about the Creator are considered to be particularly auspicious, but require honesty and humility if the omens are to be fulfiled. There is an unwritten law in the bible that God should never be physically described, there are merely manifestations of His presence such as the fire in the burning bush beheld by Moses, or the still, small voice heard by Elijah in the wilderness. Islam forbids direct representation of Allah and until the fifteenth century, Christian images of God were rare. The patriarchal figure with flowing robes and a long white beard is a comparatively late incarnation, but one that many dreamers are familiar with. God may also be represented as a radiant light, but however he appears to the dreamer during sleep His presence should always be welcomed (despite rebukes or criticism) and any message relayed is

likely to be significant—a catalyst for spiritual advancement or a reaffirmation of existing religious convictions.

Heaven is usually thought to be located above the Earth and in most cultures the words "heaven" and "heavens" have similar meaning. The perception that, through a life of righteousness the soul ascends to heaven, continues to influence our dreamscape where heaven is considered to be above the clouds or (more recently) somewhere in space. Dreams of heaven usually entail traveling within a spiritual dimension and may on rare, but fortunate occasions, involve the dreamer in a form of astral projection. This may be a life-enriching experience, which if nurtured can cleanse earthly anxieties and problems.

A far less comfortable destination for dreamers is to be pitched-forked headlong into hell. The subconscious mind's penchant for heavily underlining its messages with powerful force ensures that the sleeper may be treated to the full works with the smell of brimstone and the lamentations of the damned roasting in the fiery furnace with a host of attendant devils and demons busy about their terrible works. The vision is

the psyche's response to past worries and uncertainties that haunt the sleeper still—perhaps a shamming incident or a betrayal—and serves to guard against their recurrence. The omens suggest you have a period of melancholic reflection by way of atonement.

The devil may appear in a variety of disguises and he has long been part of our dreamscape. To glimpse him in sleep was considered by Victorian almanacs to be a forerunner of despair, though more recent thought suggests the devil may represent an authoritarian figure, possibly due to the incompatibility of adolescents with their parents. Indeed, the omens concerning the devil's presence within the realms of sleep remain slightly ambiguous and it may be argued that he is a servant of God, as he forewarns and punishes sin.

Church and Church Furnishings

Dreams involving churches or temples are obviously influenced by the ideology of the sleeper. Even for those whose faith is weak or nonexistent, the vision of such buildings are frequently an omen of solace. They should be seen as a signal to acknowledge spiritual conflicts within

association. Baptism, the spiritual cleansing and acceptance into the Christian faith, occurs at the font. Many are eight-sided—the number of regeneration—and the symbolism of a circular bowl containing the spiritual element of water predates Christianity by several thousand years. The font, as an omen in dreamlore, points to aspects of renewal and redirection and forecast a sudden widening of horizons within the sleeper's life. The altar is the focal point of most church services and is the highest and holiest (both literally and figuratively) place within the building. To dream of an altar, or sepulcher may indicate a forthcoming marriage, though some sources speak of its symbolism as a caution against committing evil. To be seen with your back to the altar warns of impending humiliation or disgrace due to a secret desire.

Dreaming that you hear the joyous sound of church bells indicates the imminent arrival of good news. However, if a solitary bell is imagined tolling a somber note, the omen warns of difficulties in the months to follow. Similarly, to hear cheerful music played on a church organ or sung by a choir,

the dreamer and they should seek to remedy it by adopting a more enlightened approach to life. A church could also represent sanctuary. The dreamer should try to work out what they fear and why they are running away from it.

Two objects often recorded in dreams are the font and the altar and both are highly charged with symbolic

foretells encouraging times ahead, but a gloomy recital or dirge-like song reverses the prophecy. Whatever music you hear in a dream evokes its own resonance.

A gargoyle may seem to be an unlikely companion in a dream, yet its presence is almost a dream of contrary. These unusually ugly creations of vivid medieval imagining, were conjured up by stone masons to adorn the walls of cathedrals and churches on the premise that evil can drive away evil. The more hideous the statues seem, the greater is their power to protect or deflect evil. As a dream omen, gargoyles caution against taking people at face value. True worth lies within a person's heart and is not to be judged lightly.

Symbols of Faith

The sign of the cross was a sacred symbol long before the advent of Christianity and was carved into domestic stonework or worn around the necks of men and cattle as an amulet to ward away evil influences. It was not until two hundred years after the execution of Christ that the symbol started to become popular among Christians. It was a further one hundred years before it was officially allowed to stand as a symbol of Christ's passion. To see a cross in your dream may represent contentment and wellbeing as an echo of the protective talisman of folk-memory. More probably, it represents a reaffirmation of faith and a spiritual benediction. An inverted crucifix seen during sleep may be the stark imagery your psyche uses to urge the dreamer to be more open to their spiritual nature and less worldly-wise.

Dreaming that you read the Bible, or a holy book, indicates discretion and sensitivity. But to imagine swearing an oath upon one suggests you find it difficult to assert yourself in matters that you feel strongly about. Similarly, to dream that you pray to God may disguise an element of self-doubt, where you rely upon the actions of others rather than stand and fight for your own cause and beliefs. Within the dream, the smell of incense in a temple or church should be regarded as a lucky talisman. The smoke of incense is linked to purity and the ascent of the spirit toward heaven. In dreams it symbolizes deep insight or a sudden revelation.

As with the symbolism of the cross, the chalice has come to be seen as a

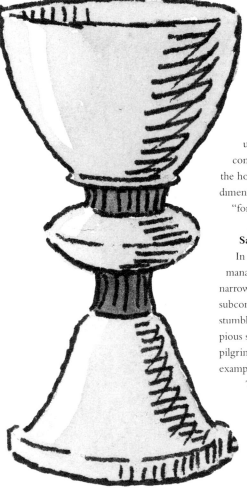

Christian icon of communion, but its pedigree as a symbol extends much further back in time. In dreamlore its ancient association with "the well of the emotions" made it a revered omen and to see the chalice overflowing suggests unimaginable bounty. The connection between the chalice and the holy grail endows a greater spiritual dimension, whereby it becomes the "font of life."

Saints, Priests, and Pilgrims

In Christian symbolism, few people manage to tread the straight and narrow path that leads to salvation. Our subconscious realizes that we all stumble along the way, but it selects the pious such as saints, martyrs, and pilgrims, to set before the dreamer as examples of our ideal self.

To dream of a saint signifies consolation and they may appear as a guardian spirit to watch over you. However, this personal protection comes with a price as their presence within your

dreamscape implies a threat of censure for your shortcomings and a warning to return to conventional values. You must live honestly and try to follow their saintly example in thought and deed. To dream of a martyr or their death reflects a sleeper's magnanimous nature. They will make great sacrifices for the ideals they believe in and so it is a decisive omen that promises much.

Embarking on a pilgrimage can be considered an act of penitence if it is undertaken in a dream. Perhaps the "pilgrim" feels guilt over some action committed in life that they wish to atone for in their sleep. The medieval goal of remitting sin by worship at the shrine of a saint or martyr is echoed by the dreamer's psyche as it seeks to exorcize past misdemeanors with the symbolism of a pilgrim's quest.

To dream of a priest or clergyman infers an authority figure that possibly mirrors a paternal stereotype. The dream implies that others are looking after your spiritual welfare; some you will know about, others you will not. A monk implies a calm austerity, piety, and withdrawal from the world and to see this omen in a dream foretells a general transformation in your life that will be greatly to your benefit. A hooded monk symbolizes healing (monasteries were among the first to introduce hospital care) and his shadowed face, obscured by the cowl of his habit, serves to add mystery to the healing process. His presence within dreamlore offers the consolation of recovery from illness and a gradual, but continual, return to full health

Myth and Magic

Our distant ancestors lived with the dangers and uncertainties of an existence that often drove them to seek refuse in beliefs that reached far beyond the horizons of reason. Their world often defies interpretation, as it dates from an age when people believed in the magical and the mythological without question. Despite the dubious efforts of established religion to impose their own credo, these earlier beliefs continue to haunt us with mysterious, half-remembered folk memories that filter into our sleeping world with disturbing, or fascinating enchantment. It is important therefore, to examine how each of the magical and mythological symbols came into being and developed, as their origins invariably define the dreams interpretation.

Heaven Sent

The two deities considered in the next few paragraphs, the virgin and the angel, may at first glance be thought to represent traditional religion. However, such is their pedigree that both predate the last few thousand years. The virgin (or goddess) was known as Isis to the Egyptians, Myrrha to the Greeks, Juno to the Romans, and latterly, as the Virgin Mary to Christians. In each incarnation she may be seen standing on the crescent moon, with a circle of stars surrounding her head. The virgin, in whichever guise she reaches your dreamscape, is always considered a favorable talisman of good fortune. Often the symbol of the virgin plays a flute or lyre and foretells a period of calmness and introspection is about to enter the dreamer's life. Alternatively, she is sometimes envisioned holding a ray of sunlight or a chalice of dew. The former represents spiritual progression, while the latter is seen as an encouragement to "awaken those who sleep in the dust (of sin)."

Angels are another celestial messenger sent to guard over us and to imagine one appearing in a dream is considered an extremely propitious sign that denotes spiritual protection and inspiration. They are manifestations of divine energy and are viewed as guardians. Their advice, if given to you in a dream, should always be seriously considered. To the religious, a vision of an angel may validate existing beliefs, while others may take solace and consolation from the thought that they have a spiritual protector who watches over them and always has their best interests at heart.

Darker Bedfellows

Along with the auspicious characters mentioned previously, the subconscious also employs sinister symbolism to address what it perceives to be the darker side of our own nature. These may take the form of demons and monsters, which we know to represent damnation—the same damnation that the unconscious mind seeks to warn against. The dreamer has a wealth of biblical and mythological demons to call upon. There may be imps from hell to drag sinners to fiery torments, demons of plague and pestilence, the "Lord of the Flies" Beelzebub, and Asmodeus demon of anger and lust, plus a myriad of minor devils in the unlikely form of toads, serpents, elves, and hobgoblins. Each represents the darker aspect of our own psyche, perhaps a fear of death or the unknown that is not confronted in waking life. If the demon or monster is victimizing you in sleep, it may help to imagine returning to the dream and to visualize fighting it. By killing your demons or slaying your monster, you may eventually hope to resolve your innermost fears.

The psyche may also employ figures from folk-legend to impart meaning to dreams. Werewolves and vampires may be thought of as a recent phenomenon (due to their current vogue in films and the print media), yet they have been regarded as dark forces of the night since medieval times. Both share a similarity with the Incubus and the Succubus, whose activities drain the

victim of their vital essence. To imagine either a werewolf or a vampire in your dream should be taken as a serious caution to distance yourself from someone, who through their constant demanding behavior may be slowly grinding your spirit down and draining you of your spiritual life blood.

The Ancient Assyrians first recorded ghosts in their dreamlore and virtually every generation since has looked upon their presence as an omen of good fortune. You need never be afraid of a ghostly visitation (however daunting it might appear) and you should try to heed any advice offered, especially if it concerns something that the dreamer may already be worrying about. Images of those who have passed on can impart consolation and among the most cherished visions are those in which a much loved relative returns to the dreamscape of the sleeper.

Visitors from Strange Lands

Early civilisations had little difficulty in accepting that there were few barriers between the spiritual world and that of nature. The mating of gods and humans or even gods and animals occurs in most mythologies and has given us the fabled realms of giants and ogres or the miniature world of sprites and fairies or even the amalgamation of land and sea, personified in the legend of the mermaid.

An encounter with an ogre or a giant in a dream always presages an uphill struggle against the odds. The larger the giant or more ferocious the ogre the greater will be the endeavor required to overcome the obstacle that impedes the sleeper's progress. The dream's symbolism links these factors to our view of the world when we were young (parents seem enormous to a small child and teachers or boisterous playmates may appear fearsome) and lay bare our earliest insecurities to reveal the dreamer's current lack of self-confidence.

It is said that fairies can only be seen in the twinkling of an eye or between one blink and the next. Their enchanted world is made familiar to us by fairy stories and children's books. This image of butterfly-winged innocence is, however, a deceptive one that ignores the fairy's traditional malevolence toward mankind. In dreams old beliefs linger and fairies are regarded as untrustworthy beings despite their

omen than those relating to the "little folk." The sea temptress combines beauty with vanity (symbolized by her traditional long hair, comb, and hand-mirror) and lures sailors to their doom. For male dreamers she represents a vision of the idealized woman, who he feels he could love, but who he knows will reject and ultimately destroy him. To dream that you follow her siren song, suggests shallow will-power that is easily misled by base passions. In a woman's dream, the mermaid is usually thought to represent a rival in love, whose manifest mystery and charm she cannot hope to rival.

beguiling appearance and even the best of them are considered to foreshadow trouble. What may seem to be passing pleasure signifies malevolence, a trait underlined by their favorite trick of using gold and rubies to entice mortals away from their beds at night.

To dream of a mermaid may be considered only a fractionally better

The Fantastic Ark

Mythological birds and fabled beasts have been dream companions throughout the centuries. Originally they were thought to be living creatures and were exalted accordingly. Even now, when modern man realizes their true provenance, the fantastic ark of the supernatural still has the resonance to haunt our dreams and calls upon the symbolism that dwells therein.

The dragon is the most potent animal of dreamlore and is seen as neither good nor evil, but symbolizes the primal energy upholding the material world. It carries the paradox of mutual dependency: light and dark, creation and destruction, the male and the female. The dragon embodies the union of opposites and within its being embraces the four elemental forces: fire in its breath, air as it uses its wings, water because of its sea serpent scales, and earth as it dwells in deep caverns. To encounter a dragon in sleep indicates great riches and treasures. However, the omens are totally under the control of the dreamer to use for good or for ill. The treasure is seldom likely to be wealth (foreboding greed and illusive happiness), but probably

represents an inner strength and vision that the dreamer can draw upon to overcome fear and conquer doubt.

To imagine you see a sphinx in your dream, symbolizes mystery and divinity, but its duel nature (as befits the hybrid union of human and animal form) is also an omen to beware the lure of cruelty and erotic obsession. Another amalgam of beasts, the griffin, is said to denote vigilance and vengeance, combining the attributes of the eagle (the element of air) with that of the lion (a guardian of fire). To dream of the creature is generally a caution to prevent your heart from ruling your head, lest by your fiery temper you lose a loyal and trustworthy friend.

In dreams, the phoenix is said to be an omen foretelling a fresh start and exciting opportunities that lie ahead. The bird of mythology lived alone for five hundred years, then sang its final song upon a nest made of precious spices, an aromatic funeral pyre ignited by the sun's rays. A worm emerged from the still-glowing embers, the embryo of the reborn phoenix. Its symbolism is associated with alchemy and resurrection and the bird's appearance within the dreamscape points to a fresh

beginning, possibly with a partner who will rejuvenate the sleeper both emotionally and spiritually.

Just as the phoenix is reborn in fire, the water-based equivalent is the Ouroboros—the snake that swallows its own tail. It brings together the symbolism of the circle and the serpent, and in dreamlore has a special poignancy for the bereaved, as it represents the round of existence and the continuation of the soul after death. The Ouroborus is also a famous example of creative dreaming, after the German chemist Friedrich Kekule visualized the molecular structure of benzene in his sleep as a carbon ring "like a serpent biting its tail."

The centaur, part horse and part man, combines human intellect with the characteristics of a wilder equine nature. When encountered in sleep it is deemed to caution against hasty behavior and ill-judged actions. Another legendary animal of duel nature is the unicorn, which represents the lunar and feminine, yet whose rampant horn is seen as signifying male dominance over the female. In dreams, it warns of conflicts that will always remain unresolved.

Dreams of Fabled Places

The location of a dream is an important indicator to its meaning. The setting may be the familiar and mundane, but occasionally the subconscious selects the fabulous and fabled to add weight to its message. To dream of visiting such legendary places as Atlantis or the sacred realm of Avalon denotes a desire for a greater spiritual or religious aspect to your life. You have reached a point where thoughts and ideas matter more to you than the quick-fix solution of instant gratification.

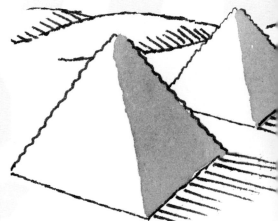

To dream of the pyramids is not uncommon and its symbolism goes to the very core of humanity's desire to understand its place within the universe. The Great Pyramid of Khufu is seen, because of its geometry, cosmology, and mathematics, to symbolize a mystery, which is as ancient as civilization itself. In dreams it is a good omen and indicates a confidence and willpower that will hold the dreamer in good stead when confronted by problems. The dreamer has the ability to conquer any challenge, however difficult it may appear.

Mazes are prevalent in obstacle dreams and their meaning is dependent upon the final outcome. Was the route traversed or did the sleeper lose their way? The classic symbolism is of Theseus (the dreamer) in the Labyrinth (the entanglement of our personal problems). To slay the Minotaur and be guided by a golden thread (your spiritual intuition) through the confusion of the Labyrinth may be seen as a victory over the debased, animalistic side of our own nature. The dream also foretells a revelation or the end of a mystery that has been puzzling you for a long time.

Magic and Sorcery

For good or for ill, wizards and witches have long held ambiguous enchantment over the subconscious mind. In past centuries, the supposed malignant influence of witches made them scapegoats for the calamities that affected society. It is little wonder, therefore, that in the realms of dreams they have come to be regarded as harbingers of evil omens and to encounter a witch foretells a rift within your homelife that could result in you becoming dependent upon strangers for support. To imagine that you fall under the influence of a witch's hex denotes that the dreamer will surrender to their baser instincts, to the detriment of wealth and personal prestige.

Wizards have little of the witches' negative connotations and are usually regarded as workers of ritualistic magic, concerned with raising their consciousness toward the divine, and gaining an element of control over the power of nature. Theirs is a wisdom born of age and experience and to visualize a wizard or warlock in sleep is symbolic of a desire to reach a higher plane of consciousness. Alternatively, a male figure in a dream relating to the occult may represent an alchemist, whose omens are invariably positive. The belief that man is the microcosm of the universe and all things in the system dwell within man, earn the alchemist a link with elemental forces and the fabled search for the elixir of life. In dreams his presence is considered empowering; driving forward a quest the sleeper may unselfishly be pursuing for the good of others.

Luck, Signs, and Symbols

Humanity has looked for omens of luck and good fortune throughout history and has sought to find them in dreams. This chapter examines the symbolism of shapes, numbers and colors, and their influence within the realms of sleep. It also looks at some of the classic examples of dream symbolism and how, by association, common and mundane objects may be elevated to prominence by our dreaming mind.

Luck and Forecasting the Future

To imagine that you have your fortune foretold in a dream, either by astrology, palm-reading, tarot cards, or a crystal ball, signify that uncertainties lie ahead. Resorting to such acts of divination indicates that you have an important decision to make in waking life. The dreamer's psyche reflects this anxiety and asks you to seek the comfort of an easy solution at the hands of a fortune teller. The omens, however, caution against such quick decision and suggest detailed discussion with those of your acquaintance whom you respect and trust.

Our subconscious mind seldom attempts to foretell the future, but merely reacts to the multitude of events in waking life that suggest paths available to the dreamer that they could choose to follow. It is similar to the wheel of fortune, which is seen to offer a great deal of movement, but by its constant turning merely returns to the point of origin. The good and the bad, the fortunate and the unfortunate, will all be equaled out over a lifetime.

Similarly, the power of luck may be regarded as circular and tends to even itself out over a period of time. To dream of being lucky may be considered fortunate, but always carries the provision not to leave too much to chance. The nature of luck (as we have seen) is always to change. Various objects have come to symbolize impending good fortune and should be noted, lest they occur in your dreams: horseshoes, pebbles with holes, the act of picking up pins, and most famously the four-leaf clover.

Lucky Numbers

It is not unusual to have a dream in which numbers appear. However, it is rare for the sleeper to remember them upon waking. If you do manage to recall the number it will be important, as each has a significance that is clearly defined within dreamlore. Symbolically, even numbers are seen as female and odd numbers are considered to be masculine. The omens and significance for each number from one to nine are examined here.

The number one symbolizes independence and the individuality of the soul. It may denote the dreamer's desire to be alone or their fear of intimacy with a prospective lover. The number two, however, represents a union of souls, the need of companionship, and a balance of the male and the female, the yin and the yang. Three is seen to be the number that underlies creation: mind, body, and spirit; the past, present, and future; and birth, life, and death. The trinity is one of the most auspicious numbers that people dream about.

The number four, when envisioned in sleep is also highly charged with symbolism. It evokes the four elements that hold the world in balance, the four seasons, the cardinal points of the compass, and it stands for order against chaos. The physical and energetic are represented by the number five, which in dreamlore highlights a wish for adventure and freedom. Six is seen to represent harmony and equilibrium: a six pointed star, the Seal of Solomon, is formed out of two triangles, one pointing up and the other down. It also encompasses creation as the world was supposedly founded within six days.

Seven is generally regarded as the luckiest number and expresses humanity's relationship with God. There are seven deadly sins that separate humanity from his maker and seven stages of initiation (the seven heavens) through which the soul must pass to stand before God.

Eight is symbolic of old age and death. In dreams it is regarded as an omen that indicates the start of something new. The number nine, when encountered in a dream, is another fortunate omen. Its power lies in the divine number three multiplied by itself—the incorruptible number of completion and eternity. Nine also denotes pregnancy and growth (the number of months in the womb).

Of all the symbolism relating to numbers, the most well-known omen relates to thirteen. In the Western world it is considered the unluckiest of all and to dream specifically of the number forebodes a series of unforeseen problems and inauspicious mishaps.

Colors and Sacred Shapes

Shape and color may be seen as male and female concepts. Form is tangible and masculine; color is spiritual and feminine, possessing the power to gladden or depress, to arouse or tranquillize. Colors tend to have an immediate impact upon our emotions and our dreams reflect this fact. If an individual color dominates the dream, its symbolism is usually significant.

The color red is visibly stimulating and stands for raw physical excitement, anger, aggression, and sexual energy. Red tells the dreamer to act now while they have the energy and motivation to accomplish their desires. Dreams bathed in an orange glow are seen to denote the hospitable and expansive aspect of

see life through intuition. They are the hues of meditation with the ability to penetrate beyond the complexities of everyday existence.

Green implies regrowth and the burgeoning of the healing process. To dream of this color when you are recovering from an illness or operation is a most encouraging omen. For those in love however, it is less fortuitous as green can also indicate jealousy. Black is synonymous with sorrow and when the color is envisioned in dreams, it may highlight the sleeper's fear of being trapped and

human nature. This color forecasts a sociable time ahead for the sleeper. To dream of the color yellow symbolizes creativity and original thinking, but also represents fear and contagion (a yellow flag was used to indicate a ship in quarantine). This dream may help to release tension by balancing the emotions with the intellect.

Blue denotes spiritual understanding and radiates compassion and peace of mind. The predominance of the color blue in a dream can liberate the sleeper from their own impulsive and reckless actions. Purple and violet are also colors of psychic awareness (combining the power of red with the sanctity and wisdom of blue) and to visualize either color in a dream highlights the need to

points to a lack of vision and clarity in their waking life. White opposes black in all aspects and the color, which represents the light of innocence and purity, possesses the energy to transform restrictions and negativity into freedom and positivity.

Geometric shapes also have input into dreamlore and to imagine a circle in your sleep calls upon one of the earliest and most sacred of symbols, representing the eternal and the infinite. To dream of a circular shape indicates a well won triumph over adversity and the fulfilment of a long held ambition. A spiral represents energy flow and in your dreamscape can point to a task that demands immediate attention and sound judgement. Squares connote stability and permanence and to visualize one in dreams speaks of security and dependability, qualities of reliability that assure the dreamer that all is as it should be.

The magic associated with the number three is also reflected in the triangle, whose shape represents the sacred trinity, a concept shared by most ancient religions and adopted into the Christian credo. If the triangle points upward in your dream, the omen should be welcomed as indicating (literally) higher things. These may be a success against all the odds or a new and encouraging lease of life. If the triangle is facing downward, however, the omens are reversed. The pentagram has five triangular-like components, and is an endless path like a circle; the union of these facets makes it a powerful occult symbol with the powers to bind or banish evil. To have a pentagram or pentacle appear in your dreamscape is regarded as an extremely positive talisman that denotes the path of safety on a perilous route.

Objects of Familiar Symbolism

The psyche may search for symbolism everywhere, but there are certain objects that the unconscious mind uses most often to convey messages. Images such as the scales, the ring, the ladder, and the hammer have familiar association with our everyday world, yet also inform the dreamer at a deeper level of intuitive wisdom.

The horseshoe is a classic good luck charm (its fortune lies in its likeness to the crescent moon) and to dream of finding the talisman foretells a charmed existence and success in the face of pessimism. To envision either an anvil or a hammer emphasizes the urgency of a message the psyche is trying to impart by figuratively hammering home the point. The louder the clang of metal, the more emphatic and urgent the message is thought to be! The hammer is also a symbol of toil and sweat, denoting lowly, but honorable work. Similarly, iron nails are said to imply the dreamer's dependence upon their own manual skills and endeavors to progress through life.

Ladders, when encountered during sleep, represent your aspiration to reach the highest rung of your chosen profession. But to imagine descending the ladder implies you may have aimed too high, too fast. A fall from a ladder indicates a lack of self belief in our own competence. To pass beneath one is considered ill luck—an echo back to the gallows when the condemned were turned off a ladder to face a slow and grizzly struggle with the noose.

The imagery of a pair of scales has been used since Egyptian times, when Anubis, the guardian of the dead, was depicted weighing a man's heart (his soul) against the weight of a feather. Only by their equilibrium was safe passage to the afterlife guaranteed. The vision of a pair of scales in a dream has a literal meaning that the dreamer should weigh up all considerations before arriving at a judgment.

Rings have been widely accepted as tokens of love for thousands of years and their symbolism enshrines the sacred shape of the circle. In dreamlore they connote attraction and fertility, but to imagine a broken ring signifies separation and heartache. If in your dream you receive a gift at the start of a new romance it foretells that your love will be reciprocated. However, gifts are usually associated with dubious luck and frequently reward your gullibility in accepting the gift by paying out in deceit and treachery.

Wells and fountains are among the most fortunate omens to encounter in sleep. They are associated with the precious gift of water and are traditionally accorded the power to heal and grant wishes. The gushing energy of the fountain symbolizes youth and the effervescence of life, while the mysterious depths of the well evokes spiritual knowledge and psychic power. To offer a token (most usually a coin) implies your acceptance of fate or luck, which in return you hope will continue to smile back in your direction.

The dream symbols of the crown, the skeleton, and the hourglass serve to show us the folly of

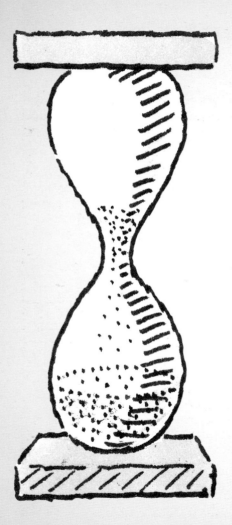

vainglorious ways. A crown, as the ultimate sign of prestige and majesty, points to the conceit of assuming to be that which you are not. Honor must be earned and never simply assumed. The symbolism of a skeleton encountered during sleep is the unconscious mind's way of reminding the dreamer of their own mortality: "All things to end are made..." while the hourglass, as the unrelenting measurer of time's passing, mocks the fleeting vanity of the moment (our own allotted span).

Sex and Seduction

F reud believed that all dreams represented our deepest desires, which in adults were invariably wish fulfilment dreams about sexual activity. Because our sleeping mind considered these desires to be offensive, our censor or super ego chose to hide their true nature through symbolism. Virtually every dream topic—from the phallic masculinity of the clenched-fist or rearing snakes to the feminine delights of unfolding rose-buds or silk purses—were viewed to be sexually motivated. However, his theory failed to explain why one night the super ego might chose to heavily disguise a sexual dream (perhaps with the image of a key inserted into a lock) while the next night it was prepared to allow a straight-forward dream of exciting erotic fantasy.

Freud's classic work on dreams built a solid base for analysis to expand, but today detractors claim that he saw sexual symbolism in too wide a range of topics. This may be true, but dreams of sexual activity occupy a large proportion of our sleeping life. They represent wish fulfilment, but can also serve as emotional safety valves or as implied reproaches against practices that our psyche considers unacceptable or obscene.

Reaching a Crescendo

All stages—from initial introduction, to
the intimacy of intercourse—carry
important symbolism in the analysis of
dreams relating to sex and seduction. To
imagine flirting in your dreams may
simply be a pleasant diversion from
normal routine, but it may represent
ostentatious behaviour that could lead
to unpleasant consequences. Flattery,
when practiced in dreams, is similarly
ambiguous, with the omens dependent
upon whether you believe in the
sincerity of the message. If you are
flattered by someone in a dream and see
it as a charming, but essentially shallow
remark, it indicates an astute and
worldly wise nature. To believe that the
flattery is genuine, however, displays a
character prone to petty mindedness
and indiscipline that will fall prey to any
unprincipled charlatan.

To imagine being kissed in a dream
may be a pleasant sensation (a wish-
fulfilment) or a loathsome event,
depending upon the person you are
embarrassing. If the dream kiss is
returned, it symbolizes joy and the start
of a new romance, although not
necessarily with the person you have
just kissed. A furtively stolen kiss is said
to lead to sorrow; an embrace with
someone you dislike is thought to
portend illness; while to dream of
kissing a partner that you are already in
love with is said to prophesy a life of
continued harmony.

To dream of confidently undressing
in front of a lover may demonstrate a
bravado that you would hesitate to
show when awake. But to be shy or
sensitive, probably reflects your waking
concern over some aspect of body
image that you do not feel at ease with.
If you dream of being seduced, it
demonstrates a willingness to
compromise too easily—in business

matters, as in love, you should not commit yourself so cheaply, or so easily.

Dreams in which you imagine making love to an attractive partner are synonymous with a hearty and robust lifestyle. However, to envision reaching a state of ecstacy displays boredom in your actual sex life, and you should be encouraged to revitalize and enliven it. A dream where you repeatedly engage in sexual activity, may simply indicate the sleeper's desire for illicit pleasures or at a deeper level their quest for a revelatory experience that is borne of both the divine and the material.

Lustful Desire

A dream in which the sleeper imagines themselves to be flying is widely and frequently recorded. It was declared by Freud to be one of the classic examples of a sexually inspired dream. Indeed, the sensation of flying can be intensely sensual (similar to swimming) and signifies a desire to enjoy a greater degree of sexual intimacy with a partner and a willingness to explore various avenues toward achieving that goal. The height attained by the flier and the ease of movement may be compared to the supposed sexual dexterity and prowess of the sleeper.

To imagine that you are invisible has long proved to be a fascinating scenario for the sleeper. It may simply indicate that you feel unnoticed by those around you, but it is far more likely that an element of voyeurism adds a piquancy to the dream, permitting the sleeper unlimited access to wherever your lustful desire takes you. Be warned, however, as the dream also carries the disturbing omen that through this deceit the sleeper should expect to discover some rather disquieting revelations and unpalatable home truths about themselves.

dealing with members of the opposite sex. This shows the twisted logic of words speaking louder than actions!

Tales of the infamy of Roman orgies have doubtless inspired dreams of debauchery, noted in almanacs over the centuries. The Victorians pronounced that such promiscuous dream images were synonymous with a man's fear of catching syphilis or a woman's concern about being labeled frigid. Modern analysis, however, puts aside these ideas and proclaims that lustful dreams of orgies serve as a safety valve to place thoughts and ideas that might be considered inappropriate within an authentic setting. It is hoped that images of excess in dreams will temper propriety and moderation during waking life.

If you feel that by some indecent or lustful action, you have brought shame upon yourself, it forebodes a bumpy emotional journey that could have long-term consequences for your honor and your integrity. Similarly, to imagine using bad or obscene language in a dream (when you do not usually employ them in waking life) indicates the dreamer's awkwardness in

Inadequacy and Frustration

Few topics provoke such unnecessary concern as those dealing with sexual performance. Depiction of the idealized sexual stereotype leave mere mortals trailing in the wake of the media's exaggerated versions of perfection. Little wonder, therefore, that perceived inadequacies enter our dreamscape with monotonous regularity. A typical example may be a dream in which the sleeper becomes embroiled in some mechanical aspect of the sexual process that causes them embarrassment or is considered distasteful or unpleasant. The dream might appear highly uncomfortable and cause concern, but rest assured, such dreams are the way our subconscious mind vents its frustration. A dream of sexual embarrassment is accepted as one of the best examples of a contrary dream, foretelling that any lover experiencing sleeping images of inadequacy and frustration can be assured of a happy and successful courtship.

Similarly, sexually impotency is another dream of opposite effect. Nineteenth-century European sources were the first to state that to imagine being impotent, prophesied a robust and vigorous sex life. However, more reserved English almanacs confided that male readers could expect simply "a favourable upturn in their circumstances."

To imagine that voyeurs watch or spy on you during love making displays the dreamer's unease with their own sexual performance and a longing to be reassured albeit by unseen eyes. Dreams of exposing your sexual organs in public places are regarded as a caution to guard against the folly of indiscretion, while believing that your genitals are deformed (a surprisingly prevalent dream) is seen to warn against the ravages of over-indulgence.

Love and Marriage

To be loved answers a universal longing and this is as true in the realm of dreams, as it is in real life. Firstly in this section, we look at the way our psyche deals with sexual archetypes and their implication for our sleeping and waking lives. We next examine the progression of romantic love, from initial attraction and falling in love, to the dream significance of courtship and the marriage service. We then go on to consider the implications of dreams relating to the negative side of love, from initial doubts and uncertainties to full-blown problems such as adultery, divorce, and bigamy.

The Anima and the Animus

From surveys of folklore and myth and his formulation of clinical analysis, Jung identified the archetypal male and female aspects of our psyche called the anima and the animus. These form a part of what he termed "the collective, universal unconscious." These dream influences have importance in forming our view of the opposite sex during sleep and by implication how we choose our ideal partner in waking life.

A woman dreaming of her idealized version of a man reflects her animus, the masculine aspect of her psyche. This is influenced by the contact she has with men, especially her father (and to a lesser extent her brothers) but this will alter over the course of her lifetime as she develops psychologically. In her early years, the animus is typically a physical, athletic man (and she will be attracted to this type of partner). Later he evolves into a romantic figure and in middle age changes yet again into a spiritual father-like figure.

The anima is the embodiment of the feminine element of a man's psyche, which manifests itself in compassion and tenderness, and a man's perfect partner might be a motherly type of woman. The anima may alternatively display its negative aspects, characterized by heartless cold calculation. Here a man could (against his better judgement and the advice of friends) fall for a lover who will ensnare him, use him, and ultimately reject him.

First Steps

The road to true love is never smooth and dreamlore reflects this. Our first faltering steps may be the realization that the sleeper is the center of another's attention. We all like to feel

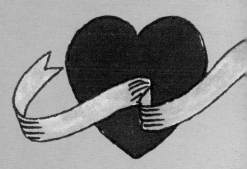

admired and in dreams to imagine this, prophesies (not unnaturally) a new romance and is taken as a sign of growing confidence and self-esteem. If on the other hand, it is the dreamer who admires a prospective partner, this can be regarded as a positive omen for future happiness, although not necessarily with the person envisaged.

You may dream that you have a sweetheart. A strangely old fashioned word, but one that perfectly matches the blend of love and innocence, personified by our first, faltering romantic steps. For a young dreamer the sweetheart may represent the perfect match, prompted by the animus (in girls) or the anima (in boys). Indeed, such may be the fond memory of our first, furtive encounters of love that its imagery continues to haunt us as we grow older and is a yardstick by which other lovers are judged.

A dream in which you imagine yourself to be in love is generally synonymous with success and reciprocated affection. If your own partner is the object of your desire, then this bodes well for future happiness, but if he or she looks pale or ill at ease, it is said to foretell a split in the relationship.

To court a stunningly beautiful or handsome partner may foretell glittering prizes or alternatively disappointment due to excessive or unrealistic expectations. Those who pursue a shy or a reluctant lover are seen to display a tenacity and assertiveness that will win them loyal friends. But dreamers who imagine they have rivals for a loved one risk losing their partner due to indecision or excessive jealousy.

Matrimony

Most cultures mark three major rites of passage in a person's life: their birth (the christening), their marriage, and their funeral. Yet of these, marriage is the only event we are likely to remember. Historically, it was the natural conclusion to love and courtship and (despite its declining popularity in some quarters) matrimony still exerts a considerable influence upon our dreams.

If you are single, a dream marriage may simply be wishful thinking. But as an omen for others, it sends out the slightly dour expectation of a quiet life devoid of friction. If you imagine a wedding in your dream, it may depict a union of opposites, reflecting both the feminine and masculine aspects (the animus and anima) of the sleeper's psyche. If this aspect of self concerns the dreamer, it is likely to manifest itself in the dark imagery of a forced wedding or a marriage to someone considered repulsive or totally unsuitable.

A marriage ceremony with someone you love is said to denote an enthusiastic approach to a new project or the dreamer's justifiable pride in an achievement. Arranged marriage, or one in which the sleeper feels uncomfortable, optimistically predicts a lively and interesting future; whereas marrying someone for their money tells of an irrational and nervous persona that clutches at straws and considers it to be support.

The symbolism of a wedding cake emphasizes the link (established by Freudian psychology) between sexuality and food. It is seen as a breaking-of-bread to bring together and unify both families. In dreamlore it may be regarded as a form of fertility symbol as traditionally a slice of the wedding cake is always retained to add to the couple's first christening cake. It portends faithfulness in love and the joyful expectation of children. The imagery of a wedding ring also has significance in dreamlore. For a wife to suppose that she has mislaid or lost the ring hints that she is becoming disillusioned with her husband; however, to find it again is a sign that her love is not wholly lost.

Uncertainties and Negative Thoughts

It is in the nature of a marriage or a partnership that from time to time it will come under strain. If the sleeper imagines that they listen to gossip and rumor about their lover in a dream, it may indicate that in waking life they are aware of some aspect of concern but which they push to the back of their mind as the possible outcome would be too painful to contemplate.

The act of eavesdropping on another's conversation is a more widely reported dream than might be supposed, although the message is usually garbled and unintelligible. The consequences of such behavior predict the sleeper is facing a dilemma which will be difficult to resolve.

To imagine that you spy on your partner is considered a dishonorable act by the psyche and rewards such thoughts with dream omens prophesying unfortunate ventures or a potentially damaging quarrel. To keep a secret from your lover in a dream denotes the need to control your passions, while to imagine that you harbor a guilty secret that may affect your romance may forebode the end of an actual love affair.

In a dream, the suspicion that your partner may be cheating on you can turn your sleeping mind to the negative emotions of jealousy and revenge. The pain of the former can consume the sleeper's spirit by gnawing at their feelings of insecurity. The omens indicate a split in the relationship or the termination of a long-standing romance. To dream of taking your revenge reveals a weak and uncharitable disposition that the sleeper should seek to control lest their lust for revenge drives one lover away and their obsessive nature make it difficult to ever attract another.

When Things Go Wrong

Giving way to temptation and, in particular, the act of adultery is one of the oldest topics in the book (or in the almanac). The uncomfortable implications of being caught and emotionally compromised may stem from some petty misdemeanor or act of folly that you may once have committed in waking life. This is the psyche replaying and amplifying your guilty secret in a dream. It might be argued that to dream of committing adultery is actually a sign of your high moral principles.

To imagine that you confess a sexual misdemeanor to your partner, invariably reflects feelings of guilt about something you may have recently done in real life. Although the symbolism regarding the confession implicates the sleeper in deceit and treachery, as with the omens for adultery, it also reflects lofty ideals and a genuine concern for the future of the relationship.

pressures accumulated throughout the day. In dreamlore, these anxieties we refuse to acknowledge are brought to the fore and given violent release and so they could be seen as a cleansing process for the mind.

To dream of being jilted by someone you love would appear to be a brutal and upsetting experience. But the dream's omen is actually the reverse and indicates the sleeper's assured success within the relationship. Another contrary dream of similar bright provenance concerns the topic of divorce which indicates that the dreamer's marriage is on a true and steady foundation, devoid of the unfaithfulness and recrimination that blight some partnerships.

Quarrels and ill-feeling can lead to a split or a break-up in actual romances and this concern fuels anxiety in the realm of dreams. However, engaging in an argument or quarrel in a dream, should be viewed as a release of

Relatives and Friends

Friends, your family, and even distant relatives may appear in your dreams. Sometimes the interpretation is obvious, but at other times it may be difficult or confusing as these people are so familiar to the sleeper. They may act wildly out of character and give the dream a surreal or even frightening edge. At other times the dreamer may envision somebody they feel they know well, but in a totally unfamiliar role. Your mother might be encountered in a dream, but as a young girl; or your son may be envisioned as an old man. These are the tricks and games our psyche plays to underline how fleeting is our allotted span. We are seen to be but a small part of some much greater plan.

Family Archetypes

Individual members of the family—
father, mother, siblings, children, and
grandchildren—each possess their own
personalities, but added to this are the
dream archetypes that forge an amalgam
to determine the symbolism of a
dream. To meet a parent in your
dream reveals a desire on the part
of the sleeper for security and
approval and they may even
imagine themselves to be a
child again to reinforce the
need to be loved and
nurtured. Mothers and fathers
are such influential characters
in our lives (even if they die
or are far away) that they defy
generalized interpretation. One
common trait, however, is their
appearance (as in life) to instruct
and support or to offer disapproval
at the dreamer's actions. This can
arouse pleasure or resentment, even if
the sleeper is an adult with children of
their own.

The archetype son or daughter of
your dreamscape is likely to be the
masculine or feminine aspect of self—
the dreamer's inner child. By observing
the child's actions and emotions you

can gauge your own strengths and weaknesses. Likewise, the aspirations of the parent (the sleeper) will be reflected in the child's achievements. The dangers and failures the son or daughter faces have repercussions for the dreamer; but their youth is a comforting bulwark against a tide of change.

Dream omens concerning siblings have changed little over the years and any dream in which you encounter a brother, or sister, is seen to symbolize courage in the face of adversity. Your burden will be lightened and your determination doubled. Even if you are an only child, believing you have a sibling in a dream is highly auspicious and denotes a strength and energy that will bring your current plans to a successful conclusion.

Whether living or dead, grandparents are seen to be a part of ourselves and without them we would not be the unique individual we are today. They come from an age that is fast slipping from memory, they connect us with our ancestors and anchor us firmly into history. Dreaming of a grandparent symbolizes security—you have those who will stand by the sleeper no matter what. If they offer

Friends and Neighbors

Dreams of friends are some of the most straightforward to interpret. If they are cheerful and robust, the omen denotes a comfortable and secure future; but if a friend appears vexed or troubled, the omens are less favorable and predict a worrying period of domestic upheaval and discord. If you dream of meeting an old friend that you have been parted from for some considerable length of time, it suggests an unease with the pace of current change and a nostalgic yearning for firm guidance and moral support.

The special bond that links friends is probably responsible for the most common example of predictive

advice, listen to it carefully and act upon it wisely, especially if you are waiting for the answer to an important question. To dream of grandchildren (whether real or imagined) indicates an appreciation of your own upbringing, but also an understanding of the spiritual duty of renewal—to connect the past with the present and the present with the future: "so was it when my life began, so is it now I am a man, so be it when I shall grow old ....the child is father of the man."

dreaming. This is where we encounter a friend in a dream who has moved a long distance away or whom we have lost contact with and the next morning a letter or telephone call from them comes out of the blue. Coincidence and chance play a role, but such occurrences are widely reported and serve to underline the close bonds of affection that link friends, even in dreams.

Neighbors may also be friends, but unfortunately some among our acquaintance provoke less positive emotions. Dreaming of neighbors has far more ambiguous connotations. To imagine you talk animatedly and light-heartedly with neighbors is a dream of contrary and predicts future troubles with these same people. Similarly, to envisage bumping into a neighbor while on vacation in a distant town or foreign country signifies a tiresome and unwelcome guest. However, to help your neighbor by performing some small act of kindness will repay itself many times over in ways we can never even begin to imagine.

Reaching Out

Occasionally the dreamer may glimpse the image of a man. He lacks emotion, and elicits none in return. The man represents an undefined aspect of the sleeper themselves (even if they are female) and he possesses those qualities of self that the sleeper values most. The dreamer's faults are also displayed and held up for criticism. Likewise, a child in a dream may emotionally reach out to you, or stir some deep sense of recollection. This is a yearning for the long gone days of your own childhood.

Children may encourage the dreamer's desire to be part of a family or they can promote nurturing feelings of mother or fatherhood. In some cases the vision of an orphan may be employed to press home the weight of the psyche's argument. If in real life you seriously consider adopting a child, this is to be warmly encouraged. However, in dreams, it may be seen as a shallow gesture of self promotion and warns against being unduly self-centered, as this will alienate valued friends.

Figures in Your Dreamscape

J ung's belief that dreams may give expression to "ineluctable truths, to philosophical pronouncements, illusions, wild fantasies, and heaven knows what beside," form a basis for his theory of the collective unconscious. This states that although the symbolism of our individual dreamscape may be personal, it draws upon a universal well of symbolism that is shared in common with all cultures, religions, and folklore. There are frequently reoccurring themes within dreamlore, as if all sleepers use the same building blocks in the creation of their individual dreams.

The figures that we select to place within our dreamscapes will to a greater or lesser extent be part of our own persona. These are aspects of our personality, which are banished to the shadows in waking life, but which the psyche may choose to highlight during a dream. The traits of our persona are woven into dream archetypes, such as the stranger, the hero, the fool, the hermit, and the wise man, who must all be regarded as images of self.

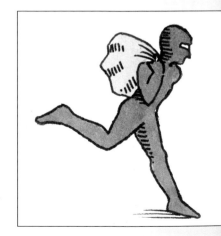

Visions of Self

Of all the figures that populate dreamlore, the stranger will be one of the most uncomfortable (and possibly frightening) to encounter, for they represent the repressed and imperfectly acknowledged part of ourselves. The stranger may also take the archetypal form of the shadow glimpsed in sleep as dark and hidden. It represents the most negative, least appealing, and most concealed aspects of our personality and the inner terrors that impel us to the worse cruelties that people have inflicted upon each other throughout the ages. However, by confronting the image of the stranger (or shadow), you may be able to examine your own character faults and guard against or improve upon them in the future.

Another facade your subconscious may employ to relay an image of self, is that of a symbolized mask. In dreams, to imagine wearing one indicates your true personality lies hidden beneath a mask and shields against expressing genuine emotions or laying bare your soul. It is a mechanism for feigned sincerity. It may also reveal a desire for sexual adventure, but indicates that you either fear the humiliation of rejection or are alarmed by the possible consequences of reckless abandon.

The wise man or wise woman is an archetype who may sometimes appear as the dreamer's parent or a figure of authority from the past. Their age denotes wisdom and they are likely to be the voice of moral rectitude, letting the sleeper know how they (your psyche) wants you to behave. It is prudent to listen to their advice, for they invariably have your best interests at heart.

A similar incarnation is the figure of the hermit, who performs the duel symbolic function of combining the loneliness of a solitary quest with the realization that only by perseverance can the dreamer's goals be attained. The hermit's guidance sets you on the road to self improvement, and a better understanding of your own worth.

The hero may be any figure—real, imagined, or from a work of fiction—that the dreamer has a particular empathy toward. But whether they be film star or action adventurer, sports personality or swashbuckling warrior, each will possess a facet that the sleeper wishes to emulate. Indeed, some analysts suggest that they may even be qualities that the dreamer possesses, but of which they are either unaware, or have not yet ventured to try.

Of all the characters within dreamlore that personify self, one of the most interesting and self-revealing is the fool. His pedigree within the collective unconscious dates back to medieval times, when the court jester was seen to possess a naive wisdom that at times made him wiser than those around him. The fool occupied a unique position, for he alone saw things as they were and not as those in authority would make believe they were. Like Socrates, he was wise enough to know that he knew nothing. To encounter the fool is to acknowledge a part of oneself that is bold enough to rely on intuition alone and can gaze in wonderment at creation. The fool advances knowingly toward the unknown; a journey to your inner self.

Inspirational Figures

A frequently reported dream is one in which the sleeper imagines that they are in conversation with a famous person. The celebrity may be living or from the past, but the dreamer will usually regard them as a close personal friend. They may even visit the sleeper's home in recognition of the special bond between them. Despite the enjoyment that such dreams may bring, it serves merely to indicate that other people may not take you seriously. There could even be a vague hint that you consider yourself inferior to others or that you feel overlooked and neglected. By associating with those you hold in high regard, you are elevated within the dream to a position of importance and can bask in the celebrities reflected glory. You are the one whom they have selected to spend their precious time with.

Occasionally, to dream of meeting a famous person can prove empowering and will add to the value of real life. To dream of helping a person such as the late Mother Teresa, for example, may actually plant the kernel of an idea into the sleeper's mind that might one day find fruition in voluntary work or charitable donation. Likewise, you might imagine yourself to be a surgeon with special skills, a musician with a prestigious talent, or the inventor of a life-enhancing product. All are dreams of aspiration and striving to achieve high ideals that can inspire and push the sleeper, quite literally, toward their dream. On a less serious note, to imagine that you create something worthwhile for the benefit of all humanity, take warning for research has found that few dreamers can remember the details of their great invention upon waking, let alone profit from their original idea.

To dream of meeting a president or even of running for high office yourself might be considered a dream come true or even a nightmare, depending upon your political point of view. The dream's portent depends upon how you rate the value of politicians in society. In general, however, the omens are not good. They forebode unprincipled falsehood and oily tongued flattery.

Those in Authority

This section assesses dreams about the "great and the good," who are perceived to have authority over us and the power to influence and mold our lives. In dreamlore they invariably represent the archetype authority figure. After parental guidance, school and teachers probably have the largest emotional impact upon a child and consequently those early years are well remembered by the subconscious. The figure of a teacher in the dreamscape underlines the need for structure in the dreamer's life. If they are seen to be giving an important lesson care should be taken to listen to their opinion for they may express approval or disapproval of current actions. Examine what lessons need to be learned.

Dreams in which the police feature are rarely the omens of trouble that might be supposed. Modern authorities consider that they symbolize protection and security and even to envisage the unfortunate circumstance of being arrested is a dream of contrary, indicating that a current difficulty will be resolved with help from an unexpected source. Alternatively, the figure of a uniformed officer in a dream might point to the conflict between the sleeper's conscience and conventional morality. It is claimed this omen suggests the sleeper feels trapped in a routine that it would be beneficial to escape from.

Issues of judgment may occupy the sleeping mind. To see the vision of a gilded statue of Justica, arms outstretched and holding a sword in her

right hand (to punish the guilty) and scales in her left (for weighing the evidence) is an auspicious omen that should greatly encourage those who face the judgment of the law. Interestingly, most people imagine that the statue is blindfolded to denote her impartiality, but correctly she should always be depicted with her eyes wide open so that justice can be seen to be done. Acting under her dominion, judges and jurors may be the subject of a dream; the omen of the former forebodes hidden obstacles that blight our path and the threat of a serious argument over some trivial matter of no importance, while to dream of jurors presages recognition from colleagues and friends for some act of moral courage or personal bravery. Rather chillingly, however, one American almanac published in the mid 1920s, declared that to dream of being a juror meant the death of an enemy.

At Home

The old cliché "home is where the heart is" may never be more apt than in the world of dreams. The home or the house (the two terms are virtually interchangeable) is probably the commonest location of all reported dreams. Home may be seen as the main stage upon which your psyche acts out its messages and everything within the house has a symbolism related to the dreamer, whether it be physically, mentally, emotionally, or spiritually.

Images of Home

As the center of most people's lives, the home is considered a fortunate omen to dream about and symbolizes comfort and inner security. As in waking life, however, niggling faults or minor problems about the house can filter through to the psyche, to be relayed as symbols. A damaged blind or a broken lock may highlight a lack of privacy or the sleeper's perceived vulnerability. A house in bad repair denotes the need to heal a family rift, whereas to dream of renovating your childhood home suggests that you should contact a parent (or parents) to resolve any problems that might exist between you both. Be aware that the nature of life is to change, so cherish that which you have while you still can. If your parents are no longer living, dreams of a childhood home may be interpreted as a regressive fantasy to a time when life seemed simpler and troubles seldom darkened the horizon.

The type of house you inhabit has relevance for the dream's interpretation. To imagine that you live in a cottage signifies a desire to escape the weariness of everyday toil and a longing for an easier life. However, if you see yourself living in a palace or a great mansion, it could indicate a conceited nature and you should be on your guard against pomposity, which if not checked will exasperate those around you. Likewise, to imagine having servants to wait upon you also foretells undue vanity.

Surrounds

If you imagine that your home is in a city, the dream is usually regarded as an omen of financial success, but at the expense of some aspect of your personal life—possibly an acrimonious legal battle or the threat of a split with a valued companion. If the house lies within a village, the omens are auspicious and prophesy the creation of a solid family foundation, and the confident expectation of a healthy and active old age.

The road in which your home is seen to be located is also symbolic. A wide thoroughfare denotes positive advancements to your circumstances; long streets caution patience; winding lanes prophesy travel and unexpected new beginnings; but muddy or rutted roads hint at obstinacy and isolation.

If the house you envisage in your sleep is surrounded by a well-tended garden full of colorful blooms and lush foliage it portends the bright prospect of well earned success and acclamation.

Such visions are often conjured up from our earliest childhood memories when, as a baby, we may have been placed near the protective security of a flower-covered wall or fence. However, neglected or abandoned gardens are dream images that forecast difficult times ahead.

Enter Within

If the garden is seen to have a gate, its aspect (whether it is open or remains

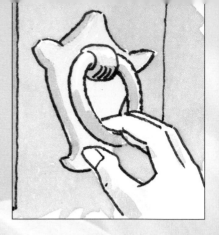

closed) governs its symbolic meaning. An open gate invites opportunities and ushers in beneficial changes for the dreamer; but gates that are shut, lock out endeavor and place barriers to impede the sleeper's relationships with those around them.

In dreamlore, to pass through the doorway and enter into a house is a decisive, symbolic action. The door represents the passage from one state of being to another and dreams can even be equated to Alice's adventure in *Through the Looking Glass*, where the sleeper may cross over into a mysterious and surreal world. This threshold (between home and the wide world) has long been the subject of suspicion and superstition. Brides are traditionally carried over the threshold and evil spirits (which have an aversion to iron)

are kept at bay by placing lucky horseshoes near the door or by driving iron nails into the surrounding frame and lintel.

If the door in your dreamscape is locked, it may represent a barrier through which only initiates, who hold the key are permitted to pass. Here, the symbolism lies with the key. Freud viewed the key as a phallus and saw potent sexual symbolism in it with the door and its subsequent opening representing aspects of the feminine. Other interpretations suggest that to dream of a key represents the unlocking of a problem or the solution to a difficulty. Its message to the sleeper is that, given time and a patience approach, problems can always be solved.

The house's other portals, the windows, may be seen to admit light or close out the world. They indicate how the dreamer chooses to view their own circumstances. Either with bright prospects that open out onto distant horizons or with an introspective outlook, marked by pulled drapes or shuttered windows.

Structures

Walls are manmade structures that compartmentalize and impose order upon our lives. In dreamlore they symbolize pent-up emotion and may reflect the dreamer's desire to break down the barriers that restrict their personal freedom. Alternatively, the wall may seem as something to hide behind, perhaps to nurse some guilty secret or conceal a lack of moral courage. If walls symbolize security, then to imagine one crumbling down or being demolished is an obvious anxiety dream. Often the wall is seen to belong to the sleeper's

childhood home, which strikes at their fundamental notion of self.

Despite widespread differences in house structure and design, dreams about roofs have changed little over the centuries. Early almanacs stated that to imagine standing on a roof foretold you would reach the heights of success, but to slip and fall indicated the achievement would be short-lived. Today, roofs (like walls) are seen to offer security and to dream of a leaking roof forebodes slowly diminishing wealth or possibly symbolizes a gradual draining away of sexual or intellectual prowess.

In dreams, stairs raise the sleeper from one state to another. The implications of going up in the world or heading for a fall are

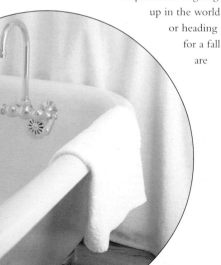

clearly implicit. Steps are an omen that you may rise in rank or authority, but to descend a staircase implies a loss of belief in your own ability. If you dream of tripping on the stairs, it may forecast problems brought upon yourself by what may appear to be meddling in the affairs of other people. You should not get so emotionally entangled, back off and learn to become more relaxed and detached.

Rooms in the House

The room in which your psyche chooses to place a particular aspect of a dream has great significance and will prove crucial to its understanding and interpretation. Within the home, the attic is thought to symbolize the intellect and the conscious mind. Here the discarded objects that we accumulate over the course of a lifetime are stored. Rather like the process of dreaming, we can visit the dark corners of the attic (the mind) to retrieve items that we think might once again prove useful or which have sentimental value. Indeed, it may well be here that our greatest treasures are to be found. The mementos and memorabilia that connect us to the people we were at

different stages in our life.

Bathrooms in dreams are associated with purification, although this does not always represent a desire for cleanliness, but could indicate an act of atonement and a wish to wash away past indiscretion. As with all water-related symbolism, clear bath water is a fortunate omen, but dirty water forebodes shame and regret. Dreams in which a toilet appears carry a whole host of emotional baggage, relating to youthful embarrassment and angst. Their appearance in a dream represents indecision and stagnation. Yet rather surprisingly, to envision an outside toilet located away from the house symbolizes a robust constitution and considerable resolve.

Bedrooms are characterized as representing rest, safety, and renewal; but to envision an unfamiliar one may have sexual connotations, possibly alluding to the secrecy of an illicit affair. Small or darkened bedrooms may signify the claustrophobic atmosphere associated with the pursuit of such an affair or alternatively they might indicate childhood fears about being left in the dark at bedtime.

Images of the kitchen suggest the dreamer is searching for domesticity and warmth in their life, almost a reaching out for maternal affection. It may be a harking back to cherished childhood memories (either real or imagined) of a happy and harmonious family life.

This is the dreamer's ideal and current events in waking life might appear to be fighting against such expectations, making the dreamer feel frustrated and dejected. Should this be the case, try to remember that everybody has problems in life. Success or failure is determined not by the problem, but in the resolve to find a solution.

Living rooms or dining rooms may be considered the heart or center of the dreamer's world and it is against this backdrop that the psyche tends to examine the interplay between characters. Thus, if someone else is in the room you need to establish whether they are welcome visitors or if they intrude; do they threaten or are you comfortable in their company? The omens should be self-apparent.

The final room for consideration is the cellar or basement. This implies the domain of the subconscious mind and instinct. Its cold and dank interior may appear to bode ill for the dreamer but to feel trapped within, yet still manage to escape is seen to foretell a major opportunity in the near future that you will feel impelled to grasp.

Household Items

Common household objects, such as furniture or kitchen utensils, are sometimes chosen in dreams relating to the home because of the wealth of symbolism they offer. A broom is seen to represent a sudden change for the better; a literal clean sweep that removes problems with a single and decisive stroke.

Kettles have been a symbol of the hearth and home for many years and to dream that you wait for one to boil possibly reflects your tendency toward impatience and desire for instant solutions. To see a kettle boiling over may symbolize the sleeper's present mood, steamed-up and about to explode! At the other extreme, the image of a broken kettle may mirror feelings of emptiness, as though all zest for life has been drained from within.

Primeval concerns for the provision of food and drink have filtered down through the ages to reach us today in many guises. Once of the most familiar is the symbolism of the cup and the dish, which forecasts providence by the level of their contents. A full cup or a well-charged dish indicates the advent of a favorable and prosperous period; but if the cup is seen to be empty or the dish smashed, then the omens are reversed and forebode difficulty and disappointment.

Candles and lamps symbolize another essential requirement from humanity's past, the need for light. Since biblical times they have been symbolic of achievement and the spiritual rewards of contemplation. In dreamlore the omens have remained little changed over the years, despite the advent of gas and electric light. A brightly shining candle is said to represent the power of inspiration and may point to a bright future in a branch of the arts. Likewise, dreaming of lighting or carrying a lantern is symbolic of self confidence and should be viewed as an encouragement to follow your own particular star.

A dream in which a table is the most prominent object in the room is likely to prophesy the need for hard work and perseverance to achieve your stated goals in life. A chair symbolizes optimism and patience, but may also warn against slovenly behaviour or the jealousy of a close friend. To envision a chair being placed under the table is seen as an encouraging sign that indicates a new relationship with someone of the opposite sex. Although this is unlikely to be of a sexual nature, it will nevertheless prove to be an exciting and stimulating friendship.

The final household object to be considered has amassed a wealth of folklore and symbolism and offers a wide range of diverse and widely contradictory omens. To dream of scissors in male adolescence might well indicate feelings of uncertainty about growing toward manhood, where the symbolism represents a fear of castration by sharp objects. However, the dream could also be interpreted as representing feelings of being cut off from family or friends and the need to reestablish contact. For other dreamers, scissors can be seen as an omen warning against dividing your time and attention between two ambitions. You should choose which option to concentrate your energy upon.

Food and Drink

Eating and drinking occur so regularly in our waking lives that it is little wonder they often frequent our dreams. In our modern, consumer-led society, the vital role that food and fresh water play in daily survival is now largely forgotten. Meat comes from the shop never the stockyard or fattening pen and fruit and vegetables are harvested from the freezer, seldom picked or pulled from an

orchard or field. But even if we are in danger of forgetting the source that sustains us our psyche is emphatically not. It draws upon thousands of years of cultural association, where the importance of various foods are imbued with magical overtones or life-enhancing properties. This ancient symbolism finds potent echo in the dream-lore of today.

The familiar imagery of eating a meal at a table is generally considered a dream of contrary. The more lavish and splendid the meal, the greater the omens point to both meanness and poverty. The opposite is true if there is little, or nothing, for you to eat. Likewise, throwing scraps of food away after a meal is a warning against extravagance.

To dream that you are cooking, presages good news or the unexpected arrival of distant friends. However, the precise implications will depend upon what is being prepared. If you follow a recipe, it foretells that any financial worries you endure may turn out to be less serious than you originally feared. To give a recipe to a friend indicates a cool head in a crisis, whereas to receive one suggests that the dreamer is held in high regard among their contemporaries.

Feast and Famine

As noted earlier, dreams in which images of plenty are sumptuously displayed usually indicate the exact opposite of what they apparently mean. Being present at a lavish banquet, surrounded by rich and worthy guests, portends unease, suggesting possible health problems, a period of depression, or a feud among friends. Empty places at the table warn of further disappointments and misunderstandings that loom on the horizon. If you are seated at the feast but do not eat, this denotes considerable strength of character and the sleeper's willingness to defend what he holds to be right, despite the disapproval and of his peers.

To dream of gluttony and indulgence, either in yourself or in other people is never a dream to take comfort from. In many cases it is the subconscious mind venting its disquiet or disgust at dietary excess. It preaches the old maxim that healthy adults should always leave the table feeling they could eat slightly more than they already have. A fasting dream in which you voluntarily go without food for a set period of time (perhaps as some act of penitence) is interpreted in a far more positive light and heralds a decisive personality combined with a focused imagination. To be hungry or fall victim to famine is another dream of contradiction; a classic example of reversal where the greater your hunger and discomfort, the more fortune is likely to smile upon you.

The Staples of Life

This section examines the dream symbolism of food staples, those commodities that form the basic ingredients of our daily diet. Wild grains and grasses were the first crops to be sown for harvest and corn has acquired an historic status in the realms of sleep. The biblical dream that Joseph interpreted for Pharaoh took as its theme the abundance and failure of the grain harvest and the vagaries of rearing cattle. Corn's importance ensured that bread was considered "the staff of life" and in many cultures it is still considered a breach of natural law to harm any person with whom you have sat down and broken bread.

In the realms of sleep, bread expressed many of the ancient qualities for which it was honored and is now considered a dream talisman of peace and physical wellbeing. By association, a vision of kneading dough or baking a loaf in the oven are also regarded as favorable omens, and it is likely a long-standing problem will resolve itself if you dream of either.

Meat is always a difficult omen to interpret, as so much depends upon the viewpoint of the sleeper. Vegetarians and vegans may find dream images of meat unsettling, and even to confirmed meat-eaters its presence within the dreamscape is far from propitious. Butchered meat symbolizes pent-up aggression and latent anger, representing the sins of the flesh. Perhaps it is simply that red meat looks similar to our own flesh or that an empathy with fellow creatures makes it an awkward topic for dreamlore. Either way, little to uplift the spirit can be gained from dreaming of carcasses devoid of their life force. Dreams that feature potatoes represent stability in the home and earthy responses to earthy problems. To dream of planting them indicates prudence and to harvest a potato crop indicates success through the sweat of your brow. However, if those you gather are blighted or rotten, the future is seen to be bleak. Rice is another of the staple foods of life that can bode for good or ill. In the East it symbolizes fecundity, where three handfuls of rice are traditionally showered upon the bride and groom as a fertility ritual. In dreamlore, the omens remain in the dreamer's favor so long as the rice crop remains healthy. A lush rice field symbolizes ease and prosperity, but should the grains be dirty or the rice impure, it foretells the demise of a long standing ambition or the inability to fulfil an important obligation.

Honey is a very ancient dream subject (having been sought by man since Neolithic times) and its preservative and aphrodisiac qualities denote the immortality of the soul or the fertility of the body. The earliest almanacs claimed that eating honey predicted the sleeper would experience an amelioration of their problems and to collect it from a hive (a daunting task) forecasts increased prestige within the community. Modern sources claim that a dreamer who imagines giving honey to other people will hear good news from the mouth of a stranger.

Gathered nuts were another staple of early man and their significance is apparent by the presence of nut hoards interned with their dead as grave gods. In dreamlore they are thought to represent wisdom and to imagine foraging for nuts may be interpreted as a desire to gain knowledge about a particular subject that intrigues you. If the shells are empty, however, it points to a problem brewing due to an act of jealousy.

Although not a food staple, salt earns inclusion for the role it has played over the centuries in preserving food throughout the winter months. Indeed, such was its importance that Roman soldiers were paid a portion of their wages in salt—the salt-money or salary. It remained a highly valued commodity, so to accidentally spill salt was to anger providence. The omen could only be countered by throwing a pinch of salt over your left shoulder as to do so is to "throw dust into the eyes of the devil" who traditionally sits on the left or sinister side of the body. In dreams, salt is said to inflame base passion and encourage youthfull exuberance. It further warns against trying to take revenge on your enemies (if you possess any) lest in trying to make them suffer, you do yourself greater harm.

Vegetables and Herbs

Dreams involving such down-to-earth plants usually forebode hard toil, with little reward for all the labor involved. More auspicious omens may be drawn from planting vegetables (representing the quality of thrift) or from tending the fields (a sign of inner strength). If, however, you dream of cutting the heads off plants such as cabbages you may, metaphorically be tightening the noose around your own neck by gullible behavior.

The dreamer may think they have been resourceful and prudent, but given time to reflect, they will come to realize that somehow they have been duped or imposed upon.

To imagine peas in your dream could indicate an awkward decision that has to be taken, but matters are complicated because all options seem to be of equal merit. Shucking peas is taken to portend recovery from illness dried peas are symbolic of tenacity and strength of purpose, while to dream that you eat peas indicates a tongue that flatters to deceive.

Onions in dreamlore denote sorrow; doubtless an association with the cut vegetable's tendency to make the eyes water. It is claimed that to see a quantity of onions represents the amount of envy and spite that the dreamer can expect to meet over the course of a lifetime. Conversely, garlic has the smell of success about it and to imagine the cloves in your sleep foretells worldly and spiritual riches.

In dreams, tomatoes imply a mixture of good and bad luck. Indeed, the plant is regarded as ambiguous as it is a fruit, yet it is more commonly thought of as a vegetable and, being a member of the nightshade family, was originally assumed to be poisonous. To dream of picking tomatoes forebodes the risk of slanderous association, but to eat the fruit indicates the recovery of a personal item that was either stolen or lost.

Perceived as an aphrodisiac, both asparagus (with its phallic overtones) and red peppers (with its fiery flesh) are regarded in dreamlore as symbols of lust and unfettered desire. *The Perfumed Garden* notes that asparagus "causes the virile member to be on the alert, night and day," while to dream of burning your mouth on a pepper or chilli warns to moderate your licentious tongue lest you bring the "disease of dishonor" upon yourself.

To imagine growing herbs is a fortunate omen of self-advancement through hard work. They symbolize stability and wellbeing, but if the dream is associated with illness, your psyche may be prompting you to consider alternative medicine. Individual herbs

Its swelling ripeness and the luscious nature of its flesh fuel the hungry libido of the dreamer. Indeed, the association may, biblically, be said to be as old as mankind, stemming from the serpent's original temptation of Eve in the Garden of Eden. Apples are, therefore, regarded as symbols that express the sleeper's desire to fulfil their sexual potential, literally to taste the full fruits of life. The omens forewarn, however, that just as Eve was beguiled by the

each have specific symbolic meaning within dreamlore: marjoram is thought to absolve and purify, rue reflects the bitterness of loss, thyme is seen to represent "love-forsaken," while rosemary is a token of remembrance and was once placed on the graves of loved ones.

Fruits of Desire
Dreams involving fruit often have sexual connotations.

snake dreamers should be wary of the result of amorous activity, in case by grasping the proffered fruit with open hands, they let slip through their fingers that which they already hold dear.

The cherry is synonymous with voluptuous desire due, no doubt, to its resemblance to seductive human lips. In dreamlore, to taste the flesh of the cherry bodes for good or ill, depending upon whether the taste is sweet or sour. Oranges proffer similar omens and for the dreamer forecast a brief, lustful relationship, short-lived, but very sweet! To imagine lemons introduces elements of bitterness and jealousy into any dream and to peel fruit indicates the separation of lovers, the caustic ending of a once flourishing relationship.

In the East, peaches are sacred to the god of long life, Shou-hsing, who plucked them from the gardens of paradise. Dream omens echo folk wisdom and to imagine eating the fruit denotes a lengthy and fulfiled marriage or partnership. Grapes envisioned hanging in rich profusion from the vine are also talismanic and point to an affectionate union, enriched by the gift of children. Strawberries are a favorable sign indicating that pleasant surprises will come your way; for a woman they presage pregnancy and the delivery of a son and for a man to dream about them means the birth of a daughter.

Comfort Eating

The sense of self-indulgence associated with comfort eating ensures that an element of puritanism becomes entangled in the equation when the subject is analyzed. Perhaps it is out-dated morality that nags the subconscious into believing that anything which brings pleasure must be bad for you, but to imagine craving candy, chocolate, or ice cream in a dream has always been frowned upon. Childhood memories and angst are aroused by dreams involving candy. When young you may have been rewarded with the treat as a token of recognition or thanks, but now the psyche uses the symbolism of candy to forewarn against indulging in the appreciation of your own abilities in a conceited or arrogant way. You need to beware the pitfalls of becoming smug as self-flattery is only self-delusion.

Chocolate and similar personal treats are said to foretell the dreamer's fervent desire to make money, but their strong disinclination to spend it. This miserly attitude is also apparent in dreams where chocolate is eaten directly from the bar rather than breaking it up into chunks might indicate sharing. A note of self-censorship is also attached to dreams involving ice cream. It warns the sleeper to make the most of life's small pleasures, for plans and ambitions all too quickly melt away.

Drink and Intoxication

Our subconscious minds may alight upon this subject simply because the sleeper is thirsty. In dreams, the omens are dictated by the kind of drink that is seen. Is it wholesome and thirst-quenching or is it drunk for excitement and intoxication?

To imagine you drink fresh, clear water symbolizes health and rejuvenation, but to swallow hot water predicts confused behavior or forgetfulness. Not unsurprisingly, drinking stagnant or foul-smelling water predicts violent illness and contagion, while swallowing cloudy liquid is said to lead to "loosen the tongue to bluster" and "boasting about wealth without reason."

Milk is symbolic of wholesome good health, but at a subconscious level it can be seen to represent a desire to be mothered, possibly a nostalgic yearning

by the dreamer for a simpler life. Due to its color and consistency, milk may alternatively represent male energy and in these instances it symbolizes a desire for masculine power and vigor rather than a need to be nurtured. Spilt milk is never a comfortable omen as it forebodes a decline in strength, or an emotional entanglement that will prove difficult, if not impossible, to unravel.

Drinking beer or wine in moderation indicates a sensible approach in both waking life and within the dreamscape. However, to dream that you indulge yourself to the point of intoxication or unconsciousness paints an unsettling picture of decline. Drunkenness forebodes an inevitable fall from social grace and strongly hints at health worries that may need to be addressed in the near future.

Finishing Touches

To dream of poison is, predictably, not an encouraging omen. It is seen to denote that the dreamer fears others may be plotting against them or that circumstances are conspiring to cause the sleeper harm. The dreamer is probably over stressed and needs to remedy the situation. Seek the help of friends to encourage you to relax more.

Alternatively, if it is you who administers the fatal dose to another (a rival in love perhaps), it forebodes that through jealousy you will end up losing everything, perhaps even your own liberty.

If in a dream you knowingly and deliberately take poison offered to you by an enemy, it suggests an unwillingness to compromise on a matter of principle.

Rather surprisingly, however, to imagine others dying as a result of being poisoned indicates that the end may be in sight for a long-standing problem that has vexed you for years. It represents a much needed respite from

any present worries and tensions that you may have.

Entertainment and the Arts

The sensations of pleasure or pain that we experience in waking life can be mirrored with similar intensity in our dreams. Pain is likely to be reserved for our nightmares, yet dreams of pleasure are widespread and associated with activities we enjoy or find stimulating. Rapturous music, an inspirational painting, the rhythm of dance, a favorite book, or images from television, film, and theater might all find their way into the sleeper's dreamscape.

Dream Music

To imagine that you hear music in your sleep is invariably a positive omen and indicates the level of harmony that currently exists in your waking life. It suggests a relaxed and sociable frame of mind at ease with family and friends. If you dream of playing a musical instrument (even though you do not know how to play one in real life) it implies the anticipation of pleasure, possibly with a new partner—a love affair that you will remember for the rest of your life. When heard, try to gauge your reaction to the music, if pleasant and harmonious it is likely to produce similar omens for the dreamer. However, discordant or sad music promises a period of vexation in the sleeper's life.

The musical instrument that you choose to envision in a dream is also an important aid to interpretation, as each has its own distinct symbolism. To imagine that you play a piano can signify the discovery of a valuable object hidden in an unlikely place. To play badly, or out of key, indicates an anxiety that you do not have the necessary skills or resources to succeed in your chosen field, whereas to

imagine performing on a grand piano shows excessive ambition and self-delusion. Selling a piano in a dream is claimed to presage a lonely old age.

Stringed instruments have a long pedigree in dreamlore and the harp is the oldest. It has associations with Christian and Celtic lore. In the credo of the latter, it is said to represent the cycle of the seasons and passage to unknown worlds. To hear its plaintive chords in a dream is indicative of nostalgic reflection and the need to take stock of your blessings.

To play or see someone else play a lute or a guitar is an omen of imminent good fortune. The lute signifies harmony between lovers and good fellowship among friends, while the music of the guitar is likely to mean that you are in the process of successfully overcoming a present difficulty. However, to dream of a broken or stringless instrument warns women to beware the wiles of flattering words and men to guard against falling under the spell of a seductive temptress.

Playing the violin or listening to a serenade played on the instrument is taken as a message that you need to fill your life with more romance. Past experiences may have embittered your feelings toward love, but you would be wise not to let this poison your future prospects of happiness. The sound of the drum also has portent for lovers, as its beat is associated with the rhythm of the heart which is said to bring men and women closer to their instinctive nature.

To imagine that you play a trumpet instructs the sleeper to be watchful of taking themselves too seriously. Don't assume that you are protected from the misfortunes that befall others. Indeed, the brassy instrument in a dream delivers the literal message to beware of blowing your own trumpet lest by your boastful and conceited actions the sleeper alienates those whose loyalty and friendship they depend upon most.

What a Performance

This section covers dreams of the performing arts such as theater, opera, ballet, and orchestral concerts and how the audience (the sleeper) reacts to them. To dream that you play in a concert orchestra carries the obvious message that you need to keep in close harmony with those around you in order to jettison your more idiosyncratic ideas and conform to the norm. Imagining being the conductor of an orchestra implies a desire to have others follow your command and indicates an illusory success gained by dubious means.

Any kind of song heard in the realms of sleep, whether it is a sweet melody or a mournful dirge, carries its own particular resonance for the dreamer. Generally, the more cheerful and pleasant the sound, the better the omens will be. Equally, dreams of the opera are dependent upon the type of performance, either dramatic, comic, or tragic and these categories roughly parallel what the future is destined to hold.

To dream of dancing usually expresses vigor and joyfulness which allows the body to express itself by putting the sleeper in touch with the animal within their soul. To dream of dancing on stage may indicate a desire to express yourself physically, but care should be taken in case a misdemeanor catches you out in a very public way. Dreaming that you watch a ballet or dance in one foreshadows possible ill health. This may be your psyche

selecting a vigorous activity to promote the idea of taking more rigorous exercise in waking life and allowing the mind to relax and unwind from everyday stress.

To imagine yourself to be an actor or actress performing a play in the theater is generally taken to be symbolic of the superficial and a sign that your talents and inclinations are focused more toward pleasure than to hard work. Dreaming of trying to learn your lines is said to forewarn that gossip will rebound upon itself to cause dire

Modern Media

We are so reliant upon television, movies, the radio, and newspapers to deliver our entertainment and information that their reported inclusion within dreamlore has dramatically increased over the past half century. To dream of watching a movie at the movie theater denotes a weak will that finds satisfaction in the easily accomplished pursuits of life. Try to do rather than watch and live your life, not someone else's.

Similarly, television viewing indicates the need for greater personal awareness and self-empowerment. As in dreams, so too in life, try to avert your

consequences. Stage fright might suggest nervousness and insecurity about your real life capabilities and if you are sitting in a theater, it is likely that the play you watch represents your own internal dialogue played out in full upon the stage. Accordingly, the audience's reaction to the dreamer's performance with their approval or criticism of the play (your life) indicates the likelihood of success or failure in actual life. Be warned, however, to never hide behind illusion as the realities of life will always find you out.

gaze from the screen and be selective in your viewing habits. Indeed, if we are in danger of becoming creatures of habit, then perhaps the dream image of a radio may serve to indicate an alternative. To the imaginative, it may in fact prove the old maxim that radio has better pictures than television.

Newspapers have been considered significant dream symbols for over two hundred years, but their omens are invariably dictated by the message the news proclaims. Reports of disasters or gloomy tidings forebode pessimistic prospects, while upbeat headlines offer positive omens and encouragement. If it is possible to read your own or a friend's name in a newspaper, it signals a short spell of fame and enjoyment. However, newspapers caution against being misled by appearance. You should question the motives of others and resist being overtly influenced by the opinion of those who may have a hidden agenda.

The Written Word and Artistic Endeavor

A book that you read in a dream symbolizes a thirst for knowledge and should always be taken as a positive omen for anyone with creative or literary aspirations. If you can remember its title or the gist of the story, it will aid interpretation when you awake. Should the book strike a particular chord with the sleeper, it may be a hint from the

subconscious to encourage the dreamer to write their own manuscript. Everybody is supposed to have at least one book within them. However, to visualize half-empty bookshelves forebodes that the dreamer's hopes outweigh their talent.

In a similar vein, dreaming of artistic pursuits is a further dig in the ribs by the psyche to get the sleeper motivated and exploring their own talents. Dreams in which an inspirational painting or an

exciting piece
of sculpture
feature shout loudly
at the sleeper to pick up
the paintbrush or bring out the
modeling clay. A lack of talent is
excusable, a lack of motivation to
use your talent is not. In dreams,
regard any reference to literary or
artistic speculation as a gauntlet
thrown down by the subconscious,
which awaits the dreamer's response
to the challenge.

Sport and Leisure

Dreams relating to sporting activity and leisure pursuits are usually beneficial and wholesome, but are likely to reveal aspects of our competitive spirit. However, they should never be taken at face value as they rarely relate to athletic prowess, but are used by the psyche as a metaphor for achievement in your working, personal, or romantic life and your attitude to winning or losing and how you play the game.

The Ethos of Victory

To participate in team sports, such as basketball or baseball indicates emotional commitment, whereas individual activities, such as gymnastics or jogging, tend to highlight the sleeper's stamina and resilience. Whatever your chosen sport, however, to see yourself winning is always an empowering omen that should have a profound influence upon your waking life.

For a victory to be worthy of the name, it should always be hard earned. To dream of winning by cheating or competing against lesser opposition is an inauspicious trait that suggests a grudging spirit and forebodes an unsuccessful inner struggle to abandon those qualities which others find most disheartening about you. The sleeper may be able to convince their waking self that fair play is unimportant and an outmoded concept, but the psyche is not so easily fooled.

A worthy challenge is usually envisioned as competition between equals, where the sleeper is aware of rivals who seek the same high objectives as themselves. As a dream omen it is important to strive to defeat other competitors in an honest fashion and only in this way will you be assured of success. The dreamer's will to win and positive attitude will spill over from sleep into the waking world.

Sporting Dreams

Sport, as a battle of equals, has existed as a concept for less than a few hundred years. However, contests such as boxing and fencing can trace their ethos (if not their pedigree) back to the gladiatorial challenge of the Roman amphitheater and the knightly tilt-yards of medieval Europe. At its most basic, boxing is a struggle of endurance, aided by individual skill and is fertile ground for dream symbolism. To imagine that you see a prize fight or dream that you are a boxer, denotes that the sleeper will pass through a period of uncertainty and discord, where your intuitive and rational halves will be at odds with each other. Time will eventually restore unity and the dreamer will have become more tenacious in pursuit of ambitions and objectives.

Similar omens to those of boxing surround individual contests, such as fencing, tennis, squash, and judo, where an opponent must be overcome and out manoeuvred by skill and guile. When envisioned by the dreamer, they indicate a considerable sense of rationality and a strong desire to display their need for freedom and independence in a tangible way. Caution should be exercised, however, lest any triumph is perverted into the boastful trait of triumphalism.

A dream in which you play a round of golf augurs well for personal matters

and business dealings, especially if your companions are agreeable and friendly. However, to record a poor score should alert you to the possibility that jealous friends seek to undermine your credibility. If you are seen to be part of a sporting team, it suggests a pride in mutual achievement when the end result, not personal achievement, is the main factor of importance. These omens bode well for romantic encounters as your easy-going personality is eminently suited to attract future partners.

Some sporting activities may seem unlikely dream topics, but the subconscious mind selects them specifically for their symbolism. To envisage being part of a rowing crew might impress upon the dreamer the importance of collective effort, where individuals are all seen to be pulling together. To dream of being an ice skater is generally considered a premonition of troubled times ahead, where skating on thin ice councils the sleeper to be wary of overstepping the mark. To harbor the dream that you are a gymnast reveals a desire for greater self-expression, but a balance must be reached between what are achievable ambitions and what are unobtainable goals. Likewise, to dream that you perform a dive into water is taken as a sign that you have started on an irrevocable course of action that must be followed through regardless of any setbacks.

Highs and Lows

In the next few paragraphs, we look at the activities of climbing and swimming and see how their dream symbolism can be overshadowed by the unpleasant feeling of falling or drowning.

Dreams of climbing are an obvious metaphor for the personal ambitions of the sleeper as they struggle toward the peak of their profession. The tougher the ascent, the greater the eventual reward will be. To slip indicates unrealistic goals set too high, but to fall and plummet downward might well be the stuff of nightmares.

Falling and the accompanying sensation of vertigo is one of the most frequently reported dream topics and has been recorded in virtually every culture throughout the world. The act of falling is engendered by various anxieties in the sleeper's life spiralling out of control from the insecurities of the workplace to feelings of sexual or personal inadequacy. Such may be the horror of the fall that the dreamer may jolt awake in terror. If this occurs, keep calm and try to remember the exact circumstances of how and why you fell, as these will assist in deciphering the dream's inner message.

Another widely recorded dream is that of swimming the sensation of which is about as near as most people come to experiencing what it must feel like to be a bird in flight. The erotic sensation of water passing over the body led Freud (famously) to equate swimming with sexual intercourse. Feeling that your are in your element while in the water bodes well for the swimmer and foretells a long and happy relationship with your partner. However, to imagine yourself out of your depth or struggling against the tide, prophesies the relationship is floundering and in danger of going under. Indeed, the suffocation and panic associated with drowning may appear frighteningly real to the dreamer and implies that in waking life you are being submerged by forces that are beyond your control.

Games and Gambling

We now turn to less active leisure pursuits, which seemingly pose less of a threat in real life, until the dangers of gambling and the pursuit of easy money are added into the equation. To dream that you gamble and win is seldom, if ever, a sign to risk money on a wager. Instead, it is likely to portend the correct result or desired outcome of a protracted and seemingly insoluble problem. Similarly, to imagine winning a jackpot or lottery in your dreams is declared to be a case of contrary and the omens signify a period of loss or hard toil for scant reward. The underlying message that there are no quick fixes or easy solutions in life should, if heeded, serve the sleeper well.

More than a little puritanism also creeps into the symbolism of cards and dice. An eighteenth-century American almanac declared the latter to be made from "dead men's bones" and to roll them and win foretold losses far greater than the gamblers and their family could afford to bear. To lose at dice,

however, points to profitable opportunities developing on the horizon.

Playing cards purely for pleasure is regarded by the subconscious mind as an innocent pastime, but in dreamlore the old proverb, "lucky at cards, unlucky in love," seems to hold sway and to dream of holding a winning hand is said to be indicative of unrequited love. To imagine playing cards for money suggests that your luck is not holding up well at the moment and some sources urge a careful rethink of finances to any one who experiences a dream win.

Playing for high stakes at poker can imply that you are too impressionable and emotionally insecure in your personal relationships, while to play cards with strangers indicates embarrassment. However, to see and remember a single card in a dream may aid interpretation. Each of the four suits is considered to have specific meaning within dreamlore: clubs indicate knowledge and the intellect; hearts signify romance and emotional attachments; diamonds are indicative of wealth and social status; while spades represent obstacles that require endurance to overcome.

Chess pieces, like individual cards, may be glimpsed in dreams and each has fairly obvious symbolism, from the majesty of the king and queen to the seeming insignificance of a pawn. To imagine that you win a game of chess points to a highly analytical mind that may be seen by others as dull and tedious. Losing a chess match in your dreams indicates that you may have over-stretched your ability and should lower your expectations accordingly. This may afford you the chance to develop your social graces.

Get Active

The subconscious mind can be a constant worrier. It worries about

moral dilemmas and it worries about physical wellbeing. Dreams of taking vigorous exercise (when you do not usually do so) is the psyche nagging us in sleep to improve our fitness. Its logic is sound and the majority of dreamers would undoubtedly benefit from the challenge to improve their health. However, a note of caution should be made. Proceed gently with exercise at first and if you have any concerns about undertaking such activity you must seek the advice of a medical practitioner.

For a jogger, to dream about running may represent the ultimate high. You can become as swift-footed as a hare, leap effortlessly over obstacles, and feel as though you possess boundless energy. Such omens presage a burning ambition that will eventually be achieved. Alternatively, the sleeper may experience feet of lead, where your grueling lack of progress represents a very common anxiety dream, especially if the runner is trying to flee from a dangerous situation.

If walking is more your pace, it is probable that this will feature in any exercise dream that your sleeping mind chooses to deliver. To dream that you walk briskly in a determined fashion denotes progress toward a personal ambition in life and this will be achieved at the speed and in a manner of the dreamer's own choosing. Indeed, if improved fitness and its attendant health benefits are your desired goal, sleeping visions of jogging or walking are a clear statement that determination and patience will ultimately enable you to realize your dreams.

Travel and Transport

The theme of travel and journeys is a long-established tradition within dreamlore and were first recorded by the Ancient Greeks who declared them to be symbolic of the sleeper's way through life, where the final destination equates to their destiny. Whether this path through life is traveled with ease or is an uphill struggle depends upon the nature of the journey. If the route is agreeable, it augurs achievement and good health but to dream that you make the journey on foot predicts an uphill struggle with scant reward. Pleasant scenery forebodes wellbeing, while barren or hostile terrain warns against dubious companions and questions the loyalty of friends. The faster the mode of transport selected by the subconscious, the sooner dreamers will accomplish or realize their current ambitions.

Departure

Sleeping visions of travel can encompass any destination, from the mundane to the exotic and before departing on a dream journey each carries its own sense of expectancy and adventure. If the sleeper feels happy and elated, the omens appear encouraging but to feel uneasy or reluctant may indicate problems in waking life that need to be addressed, perhaps by a dramatic change of routine or scenery.

To dream that you are due to depart on a journey alone is said to indicate an intriguing new proposal or an interesting proposition, whereas to travel in the company of friends prophesies apparent financial gain. However, loss and disappointment will swiftly follow. Packing luggage is symbolic of travel, but it also suggests being burdened down with extra weight. Perhaps it is suggesting that the dreamer is encumbered by a guilty secret, which they currently conceal, but would be wiser to confess.

On the Road

Few dreams offer as clear an interpretation as those relating to paths and roadways. They literally represent the sleeper's individual pathway or destiny that leads to the realization of personal ambitions in life. By assessing the route's length and condition or the terrain through which it passes, judgements and predictions may be drawn. Walking along a smooth, straight road indicates that honest effort will be repaid by just reward. Winding pathways may appear more interesting, but are fraught with countless trials and tribulations. Rocks and boulders that mar the way forebode real obstacles in waking life that block your goals and

will have to be overcome, whereas an unknown road that you appear reluctant to travel may point to concern about an ignoble deed or act of moral cowardice in the sleeper's past.

Other details of the route offer insight into the direction in which the dreamer's life is heading. The road may be an uphill struggle, denoting problems to be found in real life or a tantalizingly easy downhill stroll with the implicit warning of a life pulled dangerously out of control. Forks or turnings along the path could divert you from the beaten track and dead ends lead you nowhere. These are cautions to guard against becoming sidetracked or wasting your time and effort on irrelevances.

To encounter a crossroads as you progress along your dream road indicates that a major turning point in the sleeper's life has been reached and a decision must be made. If the correct decision is clearly obvious, your subconscious may be telling your undecided mind, which route to follow. Take note and commit yourself to the appropriate action. Occasionally, the dreamer may be fortunate enough to glimpse a signpost in their dreamscape and they should try to read and remember the destinations as this will be relevant to decisions you make in waking life.

Dreams involving tunnels or bridges symbolize the passage from one stage of your life to the next and are likely to indicate a mental transition, as much as a physical one. It is often categorized as an obstacle dream, as the bridge's construction and state of repair or the tunnel's forbidding darkness will indicate the degree of danger or difficulty that the sleeper faces on the journey ahead. If the bridge appears dilapidated or even on the point of collapse, its omens forewarn that the dreamer needs to consider all options very carefully and a period of transition is required before they make their final choice.

Both tunnel dreams and those concerning bridges signify a connecting link between two situations and the omens are governed by whether the sleeper gets out of the tunnel or crosses the bridge safely before waking. There will be obstacles to prevent a successful transition and their symbolism aids the dream's analysis. Tunnels that collapse or cave in warn of enemies lying in wait; those that apparently have no end (no

light at the end of the tunnel) caution that the sleeper labors in vain, while anything that advances toward you, such as a train or a car, forebodes ill-luck and the potential for embarrassment. Indeed, only a dream in which a tunnel is passed through or a bridge is crossed successfully and without incident can these omens be regarded in a favorable light.

Travel by Land

The mode of transport you choose in a dream and whether the trip is made by land, sea, or air will all have relevance to its interpretation. Here we examine some of the options your subconscious mind may select for its travels.

To imagine a journey made by an automobile has many convoluted omens depending upon circumstance. To be a passenger in one indicates a desire by the dreamer to have his problems sorted out by another person, often a parental figure. To take a positive hold of the steering wheel and drive yourself (often through a series of hazards) indicates a desire to take control of your own destiny. Alternatively, to imagine that the car is out of control, breaks down, or has an

accident, respectively symbolizes the realization of a long-held ambition, an awkward or embarrassing situation, and finally, that a lost item will shortly be found in a most unlikely place.

To choose a bicycle as your preferred method of conveyance symbolizes, not so much the journey, as the physical effort extended in traveling the route. The dream may be regarded as a metaphor for how the cyclist regards life—either an uphill effort (indicating reward but only after hard work) or as downhill free-wheeling (taking the serendipitous path) with all its attendant foibles and pitfalls. To dream that you fall off your bicycle is an omen foretelling that a stupid mistake is about to be made. However, if the sleeper remounts and rides away, the consequences will be of little importance, and the incident will be looked upon as an understandable error.

A dream in which you are seen to board a locomotive indicates confidence and belief in a bright future, but to disembark from one is seen to foretell a short-lived emotional crisis. To visualize a locomotive disappearing into the distance points to a romantic split and the loss of a lover, while to imagine one passing you by at great speed hints at an expectation of danger, where none exists as the only place a locomotive could harm you is if you are on the tracks so keep out of the reach of danger and then it will keep away from you.

Travel by Sea

The sea has always been regarded as a volatile companion and to traverse its wide expanse often forebodes a worrying journey. To take to the sea in a boat may appear plain sailing, but stormy seas can spring up to indicate an unhappy change in your circumstances. If you travel alone, it could signify a difficulty in relating to the needs of other people, while to dream of missing the boat literally forewarns of a failure to grasp the real implication of events.

Any ship that is seen in your dreamscape is likely to be a representation of self and the nature of a voyage suggests the sleeper's current situation. A desire to go to sea can underline a search for independence, whereas storms and raging seas that hold the ship in port indicate a reluctance to leave the family home. Indeed, your psyche may even use the traumatic symbolism of a shipwreck to graphically bring to a close one phase of your life, in readiness for the next.

The unpredictable nature of the sea make dreams of lighthouses and harbors a welcome sight. For those with doubts and worries about a serious decision that must be taken, a lighthouse shining against the blackness of the night or as a beacon through fog symbolizes that the sleeper will make a wise decision when confronted by all the facts. A harbor is a similarly fortunate omen, indicating relief from the dreamer's storm-tossed state and guidance to the calmer waters of logic.

Travel by Air

Being a fairly modern invention, dreams of flying in an aircraft have been reported for less than a century. Their earlier symbolism was entirely negative—doubtless a consequence of their deployment during the World Wars—but the omens have now evolved to indicate swift achievement. They also carry the implicit warning that however high you may fly, there is the corresponding threat of a fall. The dreamer should beware taking undue risk or going to extremes. To be a passenger in an aircraft suggests you will receive good news from an unlikely source but if the craft crashes in your dream it is likely to presage, not an accident, but a possible setback in a romantic or financial matter.

To dream of piloting a plane is symbolic of the discovery of a hidden talent or a new found self-confidence that will pleasantly surprise you as it is a facet of the sleeper's character that they never realized they possessed. To imagine jumping from an aircraft with a parachute is said to denote a contented love life, but a difficult descent points to being disappointed by someone you once respected and thought you were able to trust. The parachute is an obvious support system for the dreamer and to jump and realize that is is not packed or will not open graphically symbolizes the turmoil of the sleeper's current life. Try to get your problems in

correct proportion, things may not be
quite so bad as they at first appear.

Out of this World

Dreams involving adventurous
exploration display the psyche's desire
for challenging new horizons. As
technology expands so the sleeper
utilizes the latest innovations to keep
pace. Dreams of space travel or
journeying in the space shuttle may be
one method the subconscious selects to
represent the dreamer's thirst for
adventure and excitement.

Although the vastness of the
universe may be regarded as the
ultimate frontier, the fact that dreams of
space exploration involve confinement
within a claustrophobic craft or capsule
suggests that such imagery is narrow
and regressive. Those with a true
imagination let their spirit range free to
wander realms untouched by mortal
thoughts as with William Blake's
immortal eye to see "a World in a Grain
of Sand."

Classic Travel Symbolism

Classic travel-related dream symbols
invariably relate not to an actual
journey but to the course and

progression of the dreamer's life, representing fate and the future. If a compass is envisioned, it is a fairly predictable message from your subconscious mind to establish more direction and focus in your life or perhaps a change of course is demanded. Try to remember in which direction the needle points as it may aid the dream's interpretation. The East denotes the dawn and the freshness of youth; the South symbolizes the exotic and the warmth of human fellowship; the West is the realm of the setting sun and of rebirth; while the North points to the shade lands of the spirit.

Maps also have clearly defined symbolism and their occurrence within the dreamscape usually denotes a fastidious disposition and one that appreciates an ordered life. Maps may occasionally symbolize the desire to roam, but are more likely to indicate a journey of self discovery. If the map is confusing, it points to a lack of self direction. The dreamer would be well advised to work out their real aims and objectives in life.

To dream of a foreign flag is symbolic of travel and if you can identify its country of origin, it might be worth considering as a possible vacation destination. White flags (despite their association with surrender) are dream omens that imply the success of a venture that will inspire you with renewed energy. Not unnaturally, red flags warn of dangers and forebode the deceit of false flattery in love and betrayal by a partner whom you may once have considered to be your most steadfast supporter.

In dreams the symbolism of the wheel is deeply significant. It represents the ever-turning, ever-changing, circle of life. In dreams of travel it serves to underline the fact that no matter how far or how quickly you progress on your journey, like the wheel, the dreamer is destined to return home to the point of origin. An anchor also represents a strong attachment to a particular place. Its symbolism in the realms of sleep acts as an encouragement to settle down (perhaps after years of roaming) and reintroduce stability into your life.

Work and Finance

Dreaming of your work may not seem to offer much respite from waking life, yet its interpretation can be among the most incisive of all symbolism, as the omens directly touch upon everyday existence. We can see how we view our own worth, how the dreamer interacts with work colleagues, and the satisfaction (or lack of it) that is to be gained from our own chosen field of endeavor. The symbolism of modern technology may have little historic pedigree or foundation within dreamlore, but the omens evoked address worries and uncertainties that have troubled mankind throughout the ages. Later in this section we explore dreams of wealth and poverty of personal finance, borrowing and loss, and the symbolism associated with the world of money.

Cogs in a Wheel

The theme of hard work has featured in dreams from the earliest times and they invariably symbolize success and achievement. For the sleeper, such omens are likely to reveal problems currently facing them in real life. If the dream overwhelms you or makes you feel like a mere cog in a wheel, then this is probably the psyche exaggerating work pressure to force a waking decision or simply acts as a safety valve to release excessive tension and anxiety.

To worry about losing your job is generally considered a dream of contrary and augurs well for future prospects. It may even hint at promotion or the move to a better and more challenging position where you will be able to exploit your talents and ingenuity to the full. However, to dream of your own promotion should be seen as a warning to avoid over confidence and pushing your luck. To imagine seeing others around you working hard has pleasant connotations and suggest a fortunate coincidence that will delight and amuse you. But if those you work with are slacking and not pulling their weight, it forebodes stagnation and a lack of willpower.

If your boss makes an appearance in your dream, it implies the sleeper is feeling uncertain or vulnerable about some aspect of their working life. If they are pleasant, it portends that you may shortly be embarrassed by an unexpected piece of news and any praise or flattery offered by your employer is likely to indicate that the dreamer has misplaced confidence in a fellow colleague. To incur your boss's displeasure, or criticism augurs stormy weeks ahead, during which time you should remain calm under pressure and never rise to the bait. A common anxiety dream is to imagine that you are late for work. This plays upon your insecurity and loss of self-confidence and your lack of punctuality is further exaggerated if your employer is seen to witness your late arrival.

The Workplace

Dreaming of the office or factory could make for a dull night's sleep, but what may appear mundane often has larger significance than their familiarity at first suggests. To dream of machinery rarely indicates production, but its intricate mechanism is used by the subconscious as a metaphor for the inner workings of the body and, in particular, the brain. If the machine runs smoothly in your dream, all is well. But rusty or broken parts of the machine may be a prompt for a possible health concern.

The nineteenth-century work ethic gave Victorian dreams about factories tremendous kudos and even today their omens are surprisingly upbeat for what must be fairly dull and repetitive work. Factories symbolize a desire to be self-sufficient and foretell that the reward for hard work is success, although only of a modest nature. Dreams of an office, on the other hand, rarely relate to business matters and are far more likely to predict changes in the sleeper's romantic or personal life. To imagine you relocate to new office premises may portend an irrevocable split with a cherished friend and to have business worries during sleep forecasts discord in the home. Should such dreams become repetitive or occur on successive nights, the sleeper is probably becoming obsessed by work and a short break would prove a pleasant distraction.

Within the office, the subconscious mind utilizes any object from which it feels able to derive symbolism and meaning. An office desk, if glimpsed in sleep, is said to foretell a fruitless discussion or a hurried decision, both of which you would do well to avoid.

Until a generation or two ago, ink was the life blood of the office and to see it spilled in a dream was said to signify that the sleeper's love was being wasted upon a person whose heart had hardened toward them. Ink spilled on cloths was thought to forebode small acts of unkindness, while smears of ink upon the fingers or face were considered the marks of avarice and jealousy. The advent of the typewriter

logical manner and explore all avenues of possibility. If in your dream you are unsure of how the computer functions, or feel uncomfortable with the running software, it may indicate a work project that currently appears overwhelming.

Communications

Letters, whether for business use or private communication, reflect that steady progress is being made and (not unsurprisingly) an important message may soon be received by the sleeper. An anonymous letter forewarns of dangers concealed from view and a black-edged envelope (paradoxically) indicates joyful news. Love-letters supposedly suggest a guilty secret and to write one indicates regret for a past indiscretion.

The appearance of a telephone in a dream may highlight the stress they can cause in actual life with their constant flow of problems that demand attention. To imagine that you hear a garbled message or indistinct voices portends small vexations that over a period of time, can grow into a major headache. Email may intrude upon the dreamscape and they share similar omens to other electronic communications—a gradual, but

prompted omens which spoke of the methodical and to dream of typing augured well on the business front, as it indicated safe investment and a sure return on your money. The current icon of today's office, the computer, enters dreamlore as a symbol that suggests the sleeper needs to examine their problems in a

relentless, build up of pressure. To imagine a combative or provocative email on your screen should caution the dreamer to question the motives of those they work with as the smiles of colleagues can often mask a hard and calculating heart.

Money and Finance

In dreamlore, money is symbolic of anything that is of value to the dreamer, such as time, health, or self-esteem. To be short of money indicates a fear of ill-health, old age, or a lack of self-worth. To dream of finding money (a very common theme) is always a harbinger of good fortune, provided it is not present in excess and should always be spent carefully. An aversion to splitting a large bill for change might suggest miserliness, but it is more likely your psyche's unwillingness to divide your energies. The note equates to your potential which is never actually spent.

To dream of giving money away, especially to charity, indicates that the benevolent side of the sleeper's nature is firmly in the ascendancy. This should translate into the dreamer's waking life as a willingness to give their time and effort to help and spend where it is

most needed. Dreams in which you see coins offer favourable interpretation. To handle coins or have them in a pocket or purse signifies rapid progress in your chosen career. However, to imagine the unlikely event of swallowing a coin, forebodes ill health and pessimistic prospects. Sadly, no almanac offers the

encouragement that the change might do you good.

To fantasize about making fabulous profits from astute investments occupy night-time dreams as well as our daydreams. However, the lure of easy money is a subject the subconscious mind has a definite opinion upon. Just as there are no "free lunches" in life, so we should guard against the prospects of receiving something for nothing in our dreams. The omens for dreaming of instant financial success give warning against letting greed rule your actions.

Getting Personal

To dream of your personal finances (and in particular your salary) is considered

to be a case of opposite. To be refused a pay rise predicts promotion or a salary increase. To imagine that you fill in a tax return is a similar dream of contrary, and augurs well for a bright and prosperous future. However, to dream that you save your money (perhaps toward a pension) sees this apparently prudent action turned on its head, and the omens forecast impending financial worries and a life that will become increasingly more constrained.

Paying a visit to a bank or dreaming that you withdraw money from one is indicative of the sleeper's current concern over monetary matters in their waking life. Banks are never a comfortable omen to envision in sleep and frequently present the worst possible forecast of loss and a struggle for solvency against the odds. A dream of bankruptcy should, similarly, be regarded by the sleeper as a warning to be cautious in business matters and wherever possible follow the advice of those who have your best interests at heart.

Wealth and Poverty

The aspirations of our waking-self are seldom mirrored by our psyche. The prospect of wealth or sudden riches that so excites us when we are awake, may be turned by the morality of our subconscious, where it chooses instead to remind the dreamer of the old adage that to die rich is to die disgraced. This implies that you should seek to use your good fortune where it will be of greatest benefit as only in that way will you appreciate true riches.

Dreams of acquiring wealth, either through lucky chance, a legacy, or an inheritance, may appear to be a dream of aspiration. But it is actually a famous and well-recorded dream of paradox, where the more money the sleeper imagines they have, the greater will be its loss. Conversely, losing your wealth forebodes an assured and comfortable financial future. To imagine giving your money away with largess implies a conceited personality, that might benefit from a little more humility in its soul.

The mirror-image omens that degrade wealth into penury also operate to turn rags to riches. Poverty may appear frighteningly real when encountered in dreams, yet however powerful the imagery, their symbolism is always one of hope and encouragement. Debts are likely to indicate a beneficial event in the near future and financial failure in a dream promises success in waking life. To dream of pawning a treasured possession spells the end of a worrying problem, such is the logic of dreams of contrary.

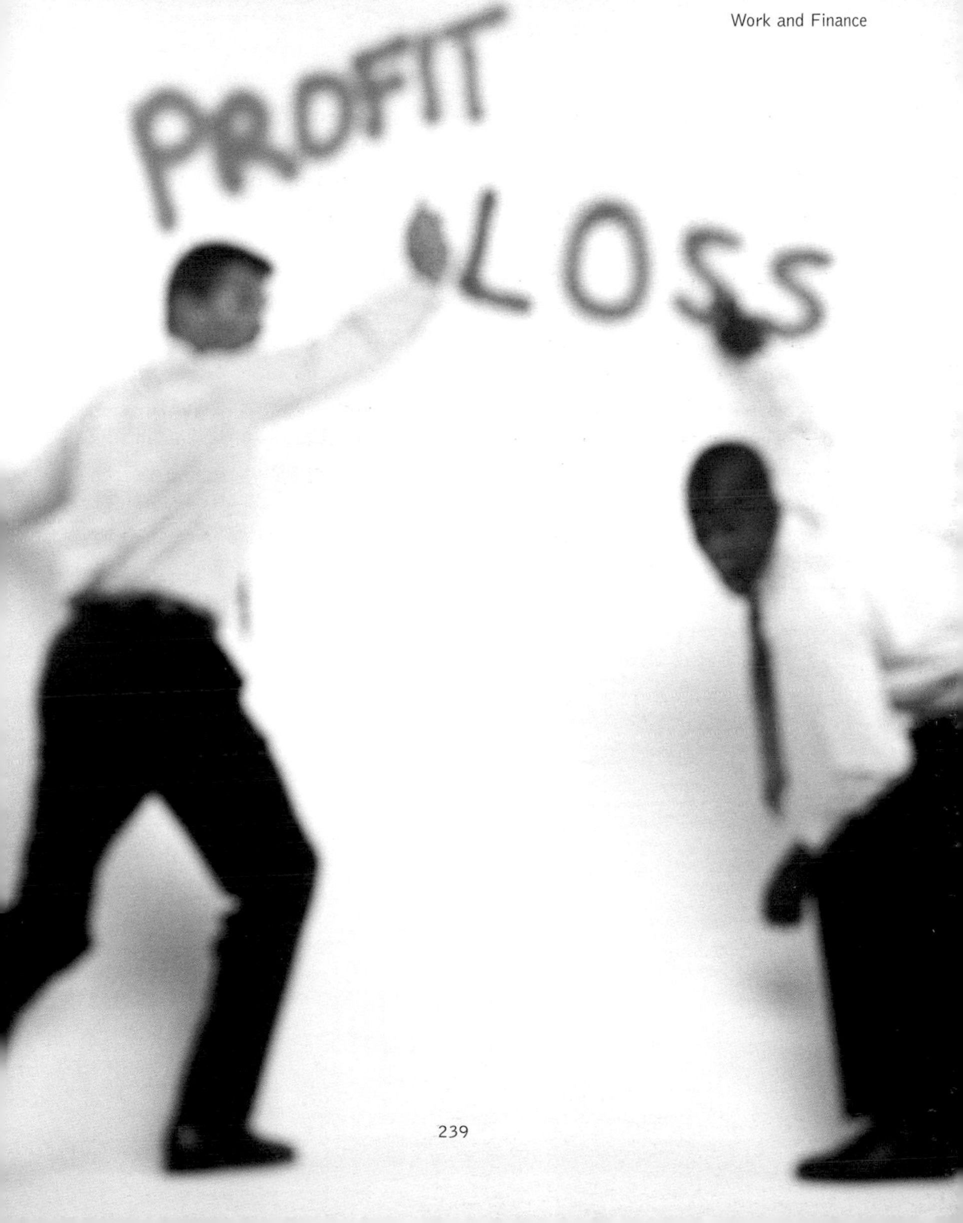
PROFIT
LOSS

War and Conflict

Dreams of violent conflict and warfare have troubled mankind since earliest times and their aggressive energies are identified with the masculine aspect of the psyche and may symbolize an initiation into adulthood for the sleeper. Despite war's disturbing and destructive nature, it can sometimes be represented as a crusade, a cleansing process that represents a victory of good over evil. However, as a dream omen, war is generally regarded as a harbinger of illness and misfortune foreboding dangerous times.

At a subconscious level, to dream of a battle may suggest inner conflicts between the dictates of the spirit and the desires of the flesh or may even warn of deep-seated grievances that need to be aired. An important aid to interpreting any dream of conflict is to remember whether you were on the winning side or were defeated. A positive outcome bodes well for the

dreamer, but to be vanquished indicates that others will ride roughshod over your plans to destroy future prospects. Rather surprisingly, however, to imagine yourself wounded in a battle is seen as a positive omen, denoting both initiation and acceptance by your peers.

To dream that you are a soldier or that you join an army may indicate a lack of discipline and structure within your life, which the sleeper seeks to rectify by association with an ordered and regimented lifestyle. Alternatively, the dream may represent a legitimate outlet for aggression with the incentive of comradeship and the possibility of heroism. Those who dream that their partner enlists for service may be seeking a more adventurous romance with the implication of a more down-to-earth approach to foreplay and intercourse.

If the conflict is at a purely personal level and the dreamer imagines that they are involved in a fight, it suggests physical confidence, a combative spirit, and an obvious need for change. However, the omens surrounding the symbolism of fighting are seldom favorable and usually indicate a loss of prestige. If the dreamer is beaten or

injured, it indicates a lack of conviction and is said to foretell that they have a serious rival in romance. Alternatively, to imagine winning the fight may symbolize a successful lawsuit or landing a prestigious contract but carries the implicit warning to be on your guard against arrogance and pride.

Fame and Glory

To imagine that you achieve fame or glory for an act of bravery is almost a cliché. Nevertheless, such themes have their own particular portent within dreamlore. Personal fame, perhaps won on the battlefield or by individual heroism, is far from auspicious and presages disappointed aspirations and a tendency toward imagined glory and pomposity. It may also represent a message from your psyche to stop striving for something which is

manifestly out of your reach. However, to dream of others achieving glory portends your own rise from obscurity to a place of honor.

If you dream that you are awarded medals, it signifies the successful ending of a time of anxiety and the ushering-in of a period of self-confidence and belief in your own potential. Now would be an opportune time to commence a project that you have been thinking about for some time. To see other people wearing medals, however, is a warning to control jealous impulses and be content with the blessings you already have.

Weaponry in Dreams

From the days of the oldest weapon—a fire-hardened, sharpened throwing stick from the Clactonian Era, unearthed on the English coastline—to the latest laser-guided smart bombs, mankind has dreamed of and worried about the devilish array of weaponry at his disposal. This symbolism is adorned with metaphor: the sword stands for justice; the arrow for speed and is an emblem of love; the dagger represents the phallus; and the scabbard embodies its feminine counterpart.

To picture a weapon in a dream usually relates to inner conflict, where elements of frustration or aggression lie unaddressed. Perhaps this is a clash between the intellect and the emotions, which often relates to the psyche's notion of sexuality. If the dreamer imagines that a weapon is fired in their direction, it suggests a timid attitude to life. You should take steps to improve your self-image and build up your levels of assertiveness. If the dream involves turning a weapon upon yourself, be vigilant for the next few weeks lest through some thoughtless action you inflict self-injury.

Cut and Thrust

To dream of a sword is symbolic of the sleeper's defence against problems and their ability to cope in a difficult situation. An unsheathed weapon is a timely reminder to control your temper and to resort to reason rather than raw emotion. To be given a sword indicates that those whom you consider friends may be untrustworthy and you should not be guided by them, while to imagine aggressively brandishing the weapon in a dream forewarns that you may be considering something misguided or even illegal.

If a dagger is drawn in a dream, it indicates the sleeper's vulnerability to enemies whom they have not yet recognized and is symbolic of deceit. To wrestle a knife from an assailant's grasp is an omen that you will overcome misfortune, but to accidentally wound yourself is the psyche's unsubtle warning to guard against your own shortcomings. To harm someone with a spear indicates a deep and bitter animosity toward that person. But to fall victim yourself to an attack is seen

to denote your own agitated and nervous state of mind. You are over-stressed and must confront problems rather than shy away from them.

According to Freud, any dream involving stabbing or being stabbed with a sharpened implement has sexual connotations of male penetration or the unsolicited, obtrusive attention of an unwanted admirer. To accidentally cut yourself in a dream may mean that problems are brewing, perhaps represented as a bad decision or an ill-advised action. Strangely, however, to wound yourself deliberately is considered an act of selfless love.

Shooting to Kill

Before the advent of gunpowder, the arrow symbolized speed and especially fate and its changeable nature. It is still an emblem of love, personified by the Greek god Eros, whose bow delivered the shot that smote mortals with love's arrows. Despite its powers to wound, the arrow is a decidedly positive omen in dreams. For those harboring a secret love, it suggests throwing caution to the wind and making known your passion. However, it carries the proviso that if the feeling is not reciprocated the dreamer must accept the verdict with good grace, and act accordingly.

Another weapon that can shoot and kill from a distance is the cannon. The weapon is viewed as an overwhelmingly masculine symbol and within the dreamscape is regarded as a harbinger of future problems, perhaps brought about by too many conflicting interests that battle all at once for the sleeper's attention. A common frustration dream is the inability to load and fire a cannon in the face of advancing enemy. The imagery emphasizes the extent of the problem, as one decisive salvo could sweep away all your problems but the sleeper lacks the moral courage or decisiveness to fire the cannon and deliver the final blow.

To dream of guns (especially handguns) forebodes trouble today and trouble tomorrow and is a most inauspicious and unwelcome intrusion into the dreamscape. To a certain extent, their shape and function mirror the phallus and thus to handle a weapon serves to emphasize the base link between violent aggression and sexuality. If you imagine you have been shot in a dream, great caution should be exercised in waking life when handling weapons and this should be doubled if you see yourself shooting another person. This is a troubling vision that hints at your own bad temper and disposition to be provoked at the slightest incident or imagined slur.

In contrast, to imagine a shield in a dream underlines a desire for personal protection, perhaps against the "slings and arrows of outrageous fortune." Whatever the shield is defending the dreamer from, its symbolism is plainly apparent and is considered a most fortuitous talisman. The sleeper stands on safe ground and any decision made by them is upon their own terms and conditions.

Crime and Punishment

Violence is a common theme in dreamlore and often results in feelings of guilt and shame when we awake. The dream imagery shows that which the conscious mind decently rejects as unacceptable. Society instills in us all the fear of punishment for acts of crime, but it cannot prevent us from having disreputable thoughts in the first place, so instead we experience these during our dreams.

Violent Ends

Here we look at the significance of what might be termed worse case scenario dreams in which we imagine acts of violence inflicted either upon ourselves or by us directed toward those we know and (in some cases) love. The first indications that such a dream is forming in our sleeping mind may be feelings of anger and rage, or even hatred, directed at a specific individual. None of these emotions are to be welcomed and each offers unpleasant omens that are likely to rebound upon the dreamer.

Dreams of anger imply that your freedom has been stifled in waking life and resentment continues to breed in your dreams. Rage may simmer below the surface to suddenly explode with violent passion and such dreams caution a need for self control in real life. Enmities and grudges poison the soul so try to avoid (as much as possible) people and circumstances that you know will make your unhappy or adopt a frame of mind where negativity cannot affect you.

To imagine that you kill someone in your dream is never a pleasant prospect but strangely it may indicate the sleeper has a need for empowerment and growth. If you see yourself murder someone you know, it may indicate your unresolved anger toward them or the elimination of some trait that you feel threatened by. Killing a parent (however reprehensible the thought might be in waking life) can signify the ending of old beliefs and behaviors, where the dreamer is killing a facet of themselves which they dislike and perceive to be outmoded. Indeed, to dream of murdering someone is rarely

an expression of violent intent, but usually implies jealousy and a wish to absorb those qualities you perceive the victim of your aggression to possess.

Rough Justice

Dreams of trial and punishment usually allow our subconscious mind to exercise the full range of its gothic imagining. Trials rarely produce justice and punishment is inevitably macabre and unsettling. To envision a courtroom plays upon the dreamer's dislike of being reproached or criticized and may give the whole experience of the trial a disturbing and surreal quality. Such dreams are said to forecast an injustice being perpetrated against a relative or friend or warn against doubtful business ventures, while to imagine being unjustly accused suggests a secret, but passionate love affair. If the defendant is adjudged guilty, it denotes the dreamer has a strong sense of responsibility in waking life and the omens are said to forecast that a venture in which you are involved is likely to have a surprising outcome.

Any dream in which a guilty party faces the death penalty is likely to be imbued with powerful symbolism and

their execution is redolent with meaning. The vision of a gallows or any other instrument of capital punishment in your sleep is probably your psyche seeking to warn you to avoid the trap of being self-righteous or overcritical. If the dreamer realizes they are the person led to the gallows, it suggests questions should be asked about the motives of those around you who have the most to gain from your impending downfall. However, to envision your own demise at the hands of an executioner is thought to be a favorable dream as death, in any form, suggests the end of a current cycle and the beginning of a better one.

Captivity

The prospect of imprisonment whether it is judiciously sanctioned or the result of arbitrary malice was originally seen as a clearly defined warning to be on your guard against treachery. But in the eighteenth century it was taken as a caution against associating with criminals and people of base instinct. The Victorians equated the pangs of incarceration with those of an unhappy

marriage, while today dreams of jail or serving a prison sentence can symbolize feelings of entrapment where the sleeper is committed to a prescribed course of action that you know will cause upset to those you love. Alternatively, the sleeper could be literally locking away some aspect of self about which they have misgivings or wish to punish.

Chains are an uneasy subject to dream about, particularly if they are used to keep the sleeper in a prison cell. They presage unjust limitations and impositions placed upon you, which can only be resolved by breaking the links. This might suggest finding a new partner or a change of employment. Conversely, to chain another represents love combined with fear and guilt and a desire to possess those who would not otherwise want to stay with you.

The psyche might imagine the punishment of imprisonment to be within a modern jail house or even a castle dungeon. Whatever the location, however, this dream is unlikely to be an auspicious one. The dream is a harbinger of ill luck and your hopes and desires are unlikely to be realized until you free yourself from the confines of bigoted and outmoded ideas. A dramatic change in lifestyle is definitely called for.

Escape

To dream that you are in despair is often the result of stressful tension that builds up over a period of time, caused perhaps by the accumulation of petty squabbles at home or in the workplace. Unlikely as it may appear, a dream of despair is also one of escape, as it is often the tonic your mind needs to trigger its release from the well of frustration and poisoned emotions.

More conventional themes of escape concern confinement or fleeing from danger. The former, escape from a

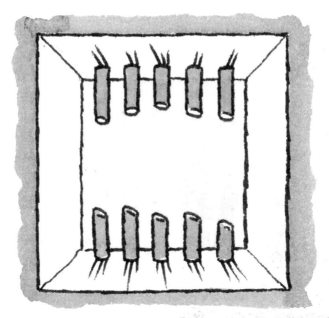

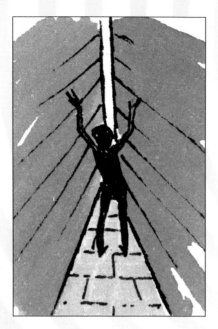

decisions and intuitive gambles. A common dream of escape is one in which the sleeper imagines themselves digging their way out of a prison cell, but the tunnel grows progressively more narrow and confining. The unpleasant sensation of being hemmed-in and trapped underground is doubtless fueled by claustrophobia and is interpreted as an obstacle dream in which success (escape) is only possible with persistent effort. To attain freedom from such confines is likely to be expressed in your dreams as a wonderfully relaxed and uplifting sensation of the spirit, perhaps reminiscent of carefree days of childhood. However, this freedom is probably your subconscious compensating for a feeling of being trapped in real life. You should try to recapture the sense of fun and wonderment that gave you such pleasure in early life.

prison, shows the dreamer has great perseverance and imagination, while the latter, fleeing from something that you are afraid of, warns against hasty

Dark Realms

In this final chapter we examine the stuff of nightmares and look at how the darker imaginings of our dreams are the most auspicious of all, having the power (if misunderstood) to hold dominion over our waking life.

In past times, it was thought that horrifying visitations in the realms of sleep were the distressing result of an "incubus"—an evil demon whose insinuations were especially directed toward young women and children,

within whom they sowed their dreams with terrifying black shapes and malignant, shadowed creatures. Alternatively, malevolent ghosts or the influence of strong, dominant thoughts specifically aimed at the sleeper by those who wished them harm were thought to induce nightmares. Various methods of protection were recommended to deflect their baleful influence, ranging from favorite prayers picked out in needlework cross-stitch hung above the bed to a crucifix (or similar religious amulet) hidden under the pillow.

Fear of predators or unexpected attack stimulated our early ancestors to make the critical choice of fight or flight, and kill or be killed. By selecting the appropriate response, our survival as a species was ensured, but with it came emotional turmoil that reflects itself in dreams. Through our fears, nightmares take on terrible magnitude but although distressing for the dreamer, modern psychologists believe that it is a healthy sign if deep-seated terrors are visualized in this way during sleep. It demonstrates the psyche's desire to confront problems that may be conveniently avoided or deliberately overlooked when awake. By arousing and venting tension we unburden ourselves of it.

Today, the stress and anxiety of daily life is acknowledged to be responsible for fueling disturbing dreams and the old notion of the incubus, who was thought to sate his sexual thirsts upon victims, is exposed as a pseudo-erotic Victorian bogeyman. Nightmares may present themselves as dreams of intense anxiety, in which we might imagine fleeing some unknown terror up a flight of stairs that wind forever upward or as a wild and violent ritual of mayhem and barbarity. However shocking your dream may appear, it is important to remember that nightmares are neither a portent of evil, nor a sign of bad fortune. In fact, such a dream (although it may seem highly unlikely at the time) can liberate and unburden your mind of worries and problems.

Our waking lives are bombarded with unsettling images of desolation and suffering, highlighted on news broadcasts or exposed through the print media. Film and television both rely upon fictionalized violence to swell ratings. This relentless flood of negativity feeds into the dreamer's existing mind–pool of irrational phobias, hidden vices, and past shameful experiences. Little wonder, therefore, that occasionally they surface in nightmares to illuminate the magnitude of stressful worries.

It is difficult to forget the images projected in nightmares and the sleeper may be startled awake (or force themselves to quit the dream) feeling oppressed and exhausted. It is only when we start to rationally think the dream through and analyze it that we begin the process of catharsis. Some of the symbolism of the nightmare will be personal to the sleeper, but other elements (such as visions of illness or death) will form part of the collective unconscious, which Jung termed symbols of transformation.

It is important to try to understand and acknowledge what it was that frightened you so much in the dream. If the issue is recognized, and subsequently resolved, the nightmare will cease. However, if a recurring bad dream (of the same theme) disturbs sleep night after night, it suggests that the dreamer's subconscious has issues that it can no longer contain and will be harder to dispel. When this occurs, it is advisable to seek out someone who you trust to confide in and share the dream with them. This will hopefully offer a fresh prospective and usually suggests a pathway to its eventual solution.

Returning Nightmares

If a recurring nightmare proves stubborn, it is often possible to "turn" a bad dream and redirect or dissipate its force. Arm yourself with the fact that, however garish or frightening it may appear, the dream images your

subconscious decides to send you are (in a convoluted way) intended for your personal benefit and they can never harm you. Try to deliberately reenter the world of your nightmare and confront the monsters of your inner darkness, armed with the knowledge that they pose no physical threat. Move them toward an imagined light, as if emerging from a dark mist, where they can be shown up as the impotent impostors they really are.

If a child is subject to recurring nightmares, where the same frightening entity scares them night after night, a helpful way to dissipate some of the dream's venom is to give the child some colored pencils and ask them to draw the apparition that scares them. Usually, they are illustrated in black or grays. Explain that the monsters love the dark and then get them to draw a strong yellow sun, radiating its light into every corner of the picture. This reduces the fear factor and confidence can be bolstered by encouraging the child to make the objects of their nightmares appear comical by drawing a funny hat on them, giving them a floral skirt to wear, or stick a joke arrow through the head. Menace seldom remains foreboding if it is subjected to ridicule and humor. The strategy may well prove empowering for adult dreamers as well.